Head for the Hills x

By

Glennyce Eckersley

Cover art by Patsy Allen

Edited by

Denna Holm

Published by

Crimson Cloak Publishing

Publishers Publication in Data

Eckersley, Glennyce
Head for the Hills
1. Non-fiction 2. Autobiography 3. Hollywood

DEDICATION

To : Val and August Bagarozzi, Arthur, Jonathan and Rob Greenberg, Sally Carlsen and in memory of Audrey and Daniel Greenberg.

Acknowledgements

To the team at Crimson Cloak Publishing, *and to my friend and illustrator of this book's cover, Patsy Allen*

Thank you to my lovely family Ross, Gillian, Mike, Rachel, Ed and Matilda. My extended family who made growing up such fun, Joan Harvey, Beryl Felstead, Philip Cooper, Ken Redfearn, Janet White, Carole Thaw and Kevin Thaw. To friends who feature in this book, Mary Bullough, Miriam Metcalf, Hazel Mannifield, Maureen Critchley, Joan Youd and Gary Quinn. Huge thanks to my circle of friends especially the 'girls who fly'. Many thanks go to The Aber family, Gloria Hunniford, Fern Britton, Dianne Nelmes of Liberty Bell, *Dyan Cannon, Richard Arnold, Becky Want, Wulfing von Rohr; and in memory of Brian Cashinella.*

TABLE OF CONTENTS

Preface

I can think of no one in my family, circle of friends and acquaintances who have not at some point in their lives visited the United States of America. I even know people who have popped across the Atlantic for a weekend to catch a show in New York. The world is certainly getting smaller by the year. By contrast however, in the early 1960s when I ventured forth across the Atlantic I knew of no one who had visited this great country. This was considered so extraordinary, that people gave me a startled look when I told them I was heading there. It appeared to be akin to saying I was going to Borneo to live with a tribe of head-hunters. Frequently the expression 'brain storm' was used to the extent that at one point I considered I might be losing my grip on reality or perhaps being exceedingly brave. An odd friend or two showed initial interest in accompanying me but as soon as passports were mentioned the reality left them very faint hearted. To me, the west of America and the golden state of California seemed like a magical place and I was determined to get there, alone as it turned out, no matter how hard it might prove to be. Initially, it was very hard indeed, but eventually it was the most wonderful experience of my young life.

I found myself in some difficult situations but fate or the angels were smiling upon me for always some wonderful person entered my life unexpectedly and saved me. Looking back this fact is crystal clear and I give thanks for the amazing people who enriched my life in those years of exploration in the Golden state. I am in fact doubly blessed because they enrich my life to this very day. My life and brush with Hollywood has been fun, inspiring, and certainly educational. Looking back it makes me smile. I hope reading these accounts will make you smile too.

Glennyce Eckersley

HEAD FOR THE HILLS

"Right, any ideas?" the voice said as I picked up the phone. It was Val with her usual Tuesday evening enquiry. Wednesday was our day off work and we would plan excitedly for a day of delight and discovery in our new city. We were, in fact, the vanguard for the European wave of au pairs arriving from England in the early sixties to work in Los Angeles. We might as well have landed on the moon, so different it was from dear old Blighty!

The journey and the arrival was an experience in itself—but more on that later. The matter in hand was the day ahead. As usual, we would meet for breakfast at *Nat's Coffee House* in Beverly Hills. The morning dawned as every morning did in Los Angeles, sunny and warm, as indeed was Nat, owner of the lovely coffee shop. Blueberry pancakes, maple syrup and a malted milk were all a revelation after the austerity of post-war Britain. We would soon learn that the breakfast contained more than our daily requirement of calories, but for the moment, we happily indulged.

Val produced a map and we debated taking a bus downtown to Olivera Street, and the exciting Mexican Quarter with its dizzying sights, sounds and smells. After a morning of this colourful scenery we could pop into the wonderful Union Railway Station, rapidly becoming my favourite building in the whole world. Its dark, cool interior was pure art deco. Deep leather arm chairs allowed you to sink into them and cool off while gazing in wonder at the departure board with its romantic-sounding names. You could take a train across the entire continent, and I longed to do just that.

Roused suddenly from my mental ramblings over my breakfast coffee and goodies, Val demanded to know what I would like to do. However, before I could reply, the decision was taken completely out of our hands.

A large car pulled up outside the little church opposite *Nat's Coffee Shop*, provoking an observation that someone was about to enter the lovely little church. Soon, more cars came thick and fast, and we realised that something special was about to happen there. Perhaps a Hollywood wedding, we convinced ourselves, and gulped down the last of our pancakes before we shot across the street. We decided to pop into the Church, hopefully without being observed. Only a couple of policemen appeared to be on duty, and a sprinkling of photographers in attendance.

Maybe, on later reflection, we managed to slip into the church unnoticed because we were dressed in black. Nobody noticed us. It was only after several Hollywood stars walked down the aisle, also dressed in black, that the penny dropped and we realized this was not a wedding party, but an actual funeral. Fortunately, we had the presence of mind to stay at the very rear of the church—until Frank Sinatra walked in and we realised that maybe we should try to get out fast.

Staring wide-eyed, and scarcely catching our breath, we struggled to take in the fact that the next person through the door was John Wayne, followed by his wife, and Audrey Hepburn. Awestruck, but trapped, we watched as the greats of Hollywood followed. Val pulled me as close as possible to the main door, where we could mercifully hide unseen behind a pillar. Clearly this was a difficult position to find ourselves in. Lucille Ball and Desi Arnaz, along with Dean Martin, were next to arrive, followed closely by the amazing Marlene Dietrich (looking smooth and tight-skinned, we wondered how on earth she moved her face. Today, of course, we know exactly how this look would have been achieved.) Eventually, the last guest appeared to have walked into the Church and so, swiftly and with considerable stealth, we sneaked out through the door.

Oh my, what a pickle we were in. The policeman, with a look of horror on his face, hastily ushered us, with a grunt of disapproval, down the steps to where a small crowd of onlookers and photographers had gathered. He told us to stay at the very side of the steps, adding that this was in fact Gary Cooper's funeral. We waited with other onlookers until the doors opened again and the coffin was slowly carried down the steps, followed by family mourners and the rest of the funeral party. The stars stood patiently on the sidewalk awaiting their cars, and only then did I became aware that I was actually standing next to Audrey Hepburn, trying hard not to stare, though she was the most beautiful woman I have ever seen. It was true to say that we did feel sad that the great Hollywood legend Gary Cooper had passed away, but we were beyond thrilled to stand and observe all the great stars of Hollywood leave that church. For two star-struck English visitors to Hollywood, we could scarcely take in the fact that we had seen everyone who was considered anyone in this town all at once. A day to remember.

That evening, after returning to my new family, I related the events with great enthusiasm and excitement. My employer listened, and then remarked with a twinkle in his eye, "It appears everyone had a good time, with the exception of Gary!"

CAT IN THE HAT

It was the hat I saw first: large, wide-brimmed and black. The old saying swiftly came to mind, 'if you can't fight, wear a big hat'. Beneath the hat was a lovely, if very stern-looking face, adorned with a pair of sixties, fashion-statement winged spectacles. They winged their way up to the forehead and made the wearer appear formidable.

"You are clearly confused," a commanding voice announced. "Are you going to Los Angeles?"

I nodded, and was at once instructed to follow the black hat quickly. Never questioning the stern voice, I followed and found myself duly checked in for the flight.

"Right, coffee time now," the voice said, and I meekly followed. Nineteen years old going on twelve, this was my first time away from home alone. Not doing things by halves, I had left the smoke of Manchester for Los Angeles.

I blame my Aunt Dorothy, who all through my early years had bought me a weekly copy of a magazine featuring Hollywood stars. It was, on reflection, the *Hello* of the day. I'd had a deep yearning to see California, and all the stars concentrated there. At the tender age of six or seven, I would stare into the mirror and comb my ear-length, mousy-brown hair over one eye and ask my mother if I resembled Veronica Lake, my favourite.

"The likeness is uncanny," she would assure me, and the die was cast. Hollywood or bust. And so, one day, it came to pass that I saw an advertisement in the *Manchester Evening News* for au pairs in California. Some enterprising chap thought he had seen the future and set up a small office in the centre of Manchester. Through a contact, he secured a few available jobs in the Los Angeles area, then sat back and waited for the rush.

A rush that was never to emerge.

Only one star-struck Lancashire gobbin took him up on the challenge. Little did I suspect that this one-eyed organisation would fold long before I had even finished packing. All this brought me to the situation where I was following the hat for a quick coffee, and a flight into the unknown. Incidentally, the flight to Los Angeles in the early sixties followed quite an amazing route. It began with the shuttle from Manchester to Heathrow, then from there to Shannon, Northern Ireland. Here we took on board more passengers and fuel before flying to Gander, Newfoundland. Airborne once more, we headed for New York, and finally across the vast continent to Los Angeles. It would have been inconceivable in those days to imagine jet travel all the way, or the future speed of a Concorde. In fact, only on one leg of the journey, namely from New York to Los Angeles, did we get to enjoy the comfort of a jet plane.

The hat sat next to me on the journey across the Atlantic. It turned out the name under the hat was Val, who at six years my senior appeared to be very worldly. She had led an eventful life to date, working in many European countries, even as a chef in Paris. I was impressed.

It had been a long tiring flight to Gander and I was relieved to hear we could leave the plane and walk around the airport during our three-hour stop. After a lovely break, we were once more back on our way, this time to New York. From there it would only be a short hop of three thousand miles to California. Feeling weary and spaced out, I disembarked in New York. This time the hat was sitting at the very rear of the plane and I'd been seated at the front, resulting in me being swept along by the human tide to the front of the queue at passport control. In somewhat of a fog, I appeared to sail through this procedure and suddenly found myself in the arrivals hall.

Had I landed on Mars? Thoroughly confused, I found the hall huge, with crowds of people dashing to and fro. I stood transfixed, clutching my ticket and completely at a loss as to what I should do next. It was at this point that another hat came to the rescue, a powder-blue pill box sitting atop a cloud of blonde hair, and wearing a Pan American uniform, the very height of glamour in those days.

Eyes twinkling and teeth gleaming, this vision of beauty asked me, "Are you okay, sweetie?"

Struck dumb, the words would not come.

She took the airline ticket from my grasp. "Don't worry, I'll make sure you find your connecting flight to Los Angeles." She beckoned a man in uniform over. "This young girl doesn't speak any English. Make sure she arrives at the correct departure terminal."

He nodded, took my elbow and steered me through the crowd. We reached the airport shuttle buses and he indicated that I should board one particular bus, explaining to the driver that I did not speak English and would he ensure I alighted at the correct terminal.

At this point it was far too late to open my mouth, so I went along with the charade. On arrival, the driver left his bus and accompanied me to the correct desk for registration. I nodded my thanks, handed the lady my ticket and passport and found myself ushered into a lovely, calm departure lounge. Mercifully sinking into a chair with a glass of water from the cooler, I began to see the funny side of the situation, especially when some thirty minutes later Val the hat came through the doors and declared loudly, "How the hell did you manage to arrive here first?"

Something like an eternity later, we landed in Los Angeles. Two sleepless nights had rendered me positively catatonic and, after claiming my suitcase, I stood watching as one by one my fellow passengers made for the exit, or were met by cheerful friends and relatives.

Val was scooped up by a lovely, elegant couple who greeted her kindly and announced they would take her for lunch to an excellent airport cafe.

Soon, the arrival hall was almost empty. No one stood with my name written on card, and no welcoming couple rushed to greet me. I sat for a whole hour on a bench trying to stay awake. After their trip to the restaurant, Val and her lovely couple reappeared.

"What on earth happened?" Val's lady asked.

"Nothing," I said. "No one appears to be meeting me."

The dear lady marched up to the desk and, after some time, came back with an angry look on her face. Apparently, she'd discovered that my would-be new employers had left a message saying I should take the bus. What manner of bus, and to where, remained a mystery. But they had left a phone number and, mercifully, this lovely lady rang them up, because I had no U.S. coins and no idea how to operate the complicated-looking phone. Val's lady gave my future employer the sharp edge of her tongue, saying she would put me on the right bus but expected them to be waiting at the other end.

I thanked them profusely as they seated me on the correct bus, paid my fare, and instructed the driver to make sure I alighted at Canoga Park. I later discovered that this was a small town out in the San Fernando Valley. Today, apparently, it is a suburb of Los Angeles, so vast has that city become. Eventually the bus pulled onto this street, a one-horse town, and I stepped out into the blast of a furnace. It was so hot I thought I'd entered the gates of hell.

Turns out I wasn't far wrong!

I stood basically asleep on my feet in the deadly heat, and told myself this was a nightmare from which I hoped to soon wake from. Actually, the night *mare* suddenly stood before me, in the form of Sheila, five-foot-two inches of bristling resentment, and a face so hard you could climb it with crampons.

"Throw your case in the trunk," was her warm welcome before driving me to the most miserable few weeks of my life.

SWINGING AT LAST

The Los Angeles Times ran a front-page picture with the headline *Party of the Year* and guess what? I was there! The party in question was hosted by the wonderful actor Lee Marvin in honour of a famous English Shakespearian acting company visiting from London. The last night of their performances was to be celebrated by a huge party at Lee Marvin's house, with more stars than you could shake a cocktail stick at in attendance.

How did my invitation materialise, you might ask? It all came about because of Leah, a new member of the English au pair girl group. We were gradually increasing in numbers, mainly due to a wonderful postman who passed telephone numbers on. Postmen, or Mailmen, as they were known in the States, drove little golf buggy-type vehicles in those days. The loud *phut-phut* noise could be heard from several streets away and I would always dash outside to greet him, hoping for a letter from home.

When one arrived, he would grin and wave the letter. "Your mom has written." Soon he became familiar with other European girls awaiting letters from home, and he thought it a good idea to put us in touch with one another. Pure genius.

Elaine hailed from the Scilly Isles, Joy from Dundee, and Leah was a Londoner. Interestingly enough, Leah was the housekeeper for an actress called Peggy Castle—who had given up her career to marry a surgeon and raise a family. Lee

Marvin lived on one side of Peggy Castle's home, and Jocelyn Brando lived on the other—Jocelyn being Marlon Brando's sister. Jocelyn Brando was, of course, a superb actress in her own right, but she was always overshadowed by her younger brother. This was an interesting neighbourhood, to say the least.

Well now, Lee Marvin and Peggy Castle decided to jointly hold a spectacular party for the English actors, and the preparations were amazing. A dance floor would be laid on the lawn, with twinkling lights hung from all the trees. A live band would play all night, then breakfast would be served to all those still standing when the sun rose. Here was the best bit: Lee Marvin asked Leah if her English girlfriends would like to come along. They would have to help serve the buffet in the evening while adding to the English atmosphere. After helping with the buffet, we would then be free to join in the party. Oh my, we did not need to be asked twice and awaited the evening with mounting excitement.

I had to pinch myself on arrival at Lee Marvin's house, seeing a helicopter pad where guests would be arriving sometime later. He was a lovely, friendly man and greeted us with a large grin. Then he took us through to his lounge where the evening buffet was being arranged. The garden was breathtaking and the evening (as most L.A. evenings appeared to be) was perfectly warm and balmy. We took our assigned positions and waited for the rush to begin.

As the first guests began to arrive, Lee's wife instructed me to take their wraps. I found myself face to face with not only all the stars from the English touring company, but also many Hollywood legends. Moving as though in a film myself, I chatted and wafted the stars into the buffet room as if I'd lived in that splendid, rarefied atmosphere all my life. The actors from the touring company assumed we were English actors residing in Los Angeles, whilst friends of the Marvins or Peggy Castle (all Hollywood stars) assumed we were part of the English touring company.

We could not lose!

What a night it turned out to be, so many interesting people to meet. I served Doug McClure, who at that point was actually Mayor of Santa Monica. He informed me he never ate cheese. John Stride, the poster boy of the touring company, assured me he did not like fish. The most interesting person there, at least for me, was the veteran Broadway and film star Martha Raye. What a character, and she was happy to chat with me as an old friend. Having been married seven times, she told me she could not help but be a comedian.

The night wore on and the dancing began. This was when, at least for me, the most surreal moment of all happened. Lee Marvin danced with me! This dance was followed by several with an English actor who had the great responsibility of being a spear carrier. He vowed his undying love and promised to marry me when I returned to England. (Goodness knows how much he had been drinking!) As the dawn arrived, we ate bacon sandwiches whilst watching the sun rise. In every sense it was a long way from cold, rainy Manchester. I had read about the swinging sixties and always wondered just where they were swinging,

At last I found out!

OUT OF THE VALLEY OF DEATH

I woke on my first morning in Canoga Park to the sound of Sheila yelling at the top of her voice. I assumed there must have been a severe problem with one of the children, though it turned out that this was the sole means of communication between Sheila and the kids. They were a mixed bunch, to put it mildly. Of the four children, two girls belonged to Sheila, but from different fathers. The two fathers were long gone and neither of the girls could even remember them. The two small boys were the offspring of Shelia's partner, and their mother never appeared on the scene either. The four did not get along, fighting day and night from the time they woke up to the time they went to sleep again.

Sheila's partner was Mexican, an aspiring film star who was convinced he would be huge in Hollywood one day. They told me that they had several shops to organise, but did, in fact, spend most days filming. Turns out he was indeed rather huge in Hollywood—more of which I'll tell you about shortly.

Still groggy and jet-lagged on my first morning, I padded into the kitchen and was handed a list of jobs for the day and told to get on with it. Sheila and partner would be home at nine P.M., and they expected a cooked meal to be on the table. Good luck with that. At nineteen, I had never boiled an egg, and so I dreaded their return that evening.

The children were picked up by a neighbour each morning for school, then dropped off again afterward. The intervening hours were to be filled with cleaning the whole house, washing and ironing, making the children's tea, bathing them and putting them to bed. Not a lot of time to sit and drink coffee or feel homesick, that was for sure.

The heat was unbelievable and I had to drag myself around this rather modest, non-air-conditioned house to get the chores done. Battling with the children to get them bathed and in bed totally exhausted me, and then all I had to do was face the wrath of the She-Devil. And, oh my, did she scream when she discovered no meal waiting for them on the table. After that, she realized they would have to resort to dial-a-meal. I was fascinated, because at the time this was something never seen in the U.K. It seemed you could order meals from around the world and have it swiftly delivered right to your door. I soon realised they had been eating this way ever since they married. I fell into bed, fatigued and miserable, facing the awful truth that the next morning, at six A.M. sharp, I'd be expected to feed the children and get them ready for school—an endless repeat of the previous day's programme. How on earth would I ever survive it?

Six weeks of pure hell followed. When I finally did get a day off, there was nowhere to go, and no one to go with. I rang the contact number of the chap in Manchester who had negotiated this position only to find the agency had closed. I was on my own. There was no one to appeal to for help. I had no money, having used all my saving for the air fare to get to California. Pride would not allow me to tell my parents, who'd had concerns enough about this foolish escapade, as they had referred to it.

It was dawning on me that I might have to spend the rest of my life in domestic slavery when out of the blue came a phone call from Val the Hat. She had kept my telephone number, and her cheery voice asked, "How are you doing, Glennyce?"

Never so happy to hear a familiar voice, I filled her in on the details of my tale of woe.

"Leave it with me," was all she said. "I will get back to you shortly."

You could only describe Val as a real Panglossian, and true to what I soon realised was her form, in what appeared to be the twinkling of an eye, Val was back on the line. She had perused her local paper and found an advertisement for a European nanny at a house only minutes from where she lived. She rung the person immediately and arranged an interview. Then she related my predicament to her wonderful employers, who were not at all surprised considering the fiasco we had experienced on arrival. Bless them, they declared they would drive out to the valley and take me to the interview. Salvation was at hand!

True to their word, they showed up at the appointed time to collect me. Eyes popping, I was driven through Beverly Hills to the equally jaw-dropping beautiful Brentwood, where I was interviewed by a warm, lovely lady for half an hour and hired on the spot.

To quote Paul McCartney, all my troubles seemed so far away.

However, on arriving back in Canoga Park, I was quaking, aware I would still need to face the full wrath of the She-Devil. Sheila did not disappoint, unleashing her full fury with language that would make a sailor blush, along with several words I'd never heard before. I still had to survive five days in that madhouse. My new employer would drive to pick me up on Saturday morning to release me from the valley. I tried hard to keep my head down for the next few days, but Sheila, thank goodness, never spoke to me again—save for the statement that I would not be receiving one penny for the seven weeks I had spent there.

One morning, in order to keep as busy as possible, I decided to clean the top of the fitted wardrobes. Finding a small ladder in the kitchen, I climbed to the top and began to dust, moving around several large boxes situated there. Lifting one particularly heavy one, I suddenly dropped it and it fell to the floor spilling its contents. I glanced down with dismay and almost fell off the ladder, shocked by the sight that met my eyes.

The box had been crammed with photographs, all of Sheila and her husband. The box label said 'audition photographs' and that's when the truth finally dawned. As my face burned bright red, I realised that they were porn stars, and they certainly were big in the film world. It was certainly quite the learning curve for a young nineteen-year-old Baptist girl who'd previously found an evening in a coffee bar exciting. Oh my, talk about innocence abroad.

At long last Saturday morning dawned, and what a huge relief. My new employer arrived with a cheery smile, and a very cute little boy on the back seat of his trendy green jaguar. As we drove away, I started to tell him something of the conditions I had endured. I also told him that I hadn't received payment for my seven weeks of employment and therefore had no money. This kind man announced that he was, in fact, a lawyer and there were a couple of things we could do. Firstly, we might sue them, but it would mean I would have to go to court. Or, he could give me an advance and I could shake the dust of Canoga Park from my sandals. I swiftly chose the advance, feeling as light as a butterfly as I headed for a new life.

My new home was wonderful and my employers could not have been kinder. The lifestyle was elegant and interesting, especially the weekends. Audrey and Arthur, my new employers, held Saturday night parties on several occasions throughout the summer. These would take place in the garden, under the stars in the flower-scented evening air. Tables were set and lights festooned the trees, until the whole place looked quite magical. For these evenings, I wore a rather smart uniform, black with a white frilly pinafore. I felt very smart. On these evenings, my first duty would be to answer the door and greet the guests, taking coats or wraps as necessary and ushering them into the lounge for drinks. I could never understand why, in warm and sunny California, women wore fur coats. On asking Audrey this very question, she laughed aloud, saying that fur was not worn for warmth and one day I would understand that fact.

Circulating with drinks on a tray, I was to ensure all the guests were served and happy. Indeed, I was quite excited as the first of these summer dinner parties got under way. As instructed, I greeted and ushered them towards the lounge, where taking my tray I began to circulate. Warm and friendly, the guests soon proved to be curious about my accent, all of them anxious to learn where I hailed from. One particular guest had, in fact, not lived far from my home in England. Soon we were deep in conversation. I was only vaguely aware of Arthur sidling up to me, sighing as he relieved me of the tray of drinks. He then circulated amongst his guests leaving me to chat.

My duties on a day to day basis mainly involved the children, but Audrey, who was a splendid cook, began to teach me how to make simple dishes to feed the children. Eventually my skills grew enough to feed the whole family. I also spent a great deal of time with Val, who had been a professional chef in Paris. She helped me with cooking lessons. However, during outdoor evening dinner parties, Audrey employed a chef from an agency to whisk up wonderful meals for sixteen guests at a time. Early in the afternoon of my first dinner party experience, our new chef appeared. Ethel was quite wonderful, a very large and very black woman with the broadest smile I had ever seen. We got along like a house on fire. I had such fun whilst learning even more wonderful recipes.

That first evening dinner party was full of surprises and unexpected events. The main course was to be a large leg of lamb, roasted to perfection. My job was to lift this behemoth leg of lamb from the oven and place it onto a serving dish, where Arthur would carve it before taking it outside to the waiting diners. I lifted this monster from the oven with great care. After taking the two large forks indicated by Ethel, I tried to lift it onto the serving dish. It wobbled and I struggled, until I suddenly lost it altogether, dropping the leg of lamb. I watched in horror as it slid across the entire length of the rather sticky kitchen floor, before coming to a squelching stop against the far wall. At that precise moment, my long-suffering employer strode into the kitchen to collect the meat. I stood open-mouthed, not having a clue what I should do next. Ethel stifled her giggles, but then to my amazement, Arthur simply scooped up the leg of lamb from the floor, dusted it on a tea towel and proceeded to slice it, giving me a wink. Without further ado, it was placed in the centre of the main table and slices served to guests. As I circumnavigated the guests with a tureen of vegetables, several were heard to say how lovely and delicious was the lamb. Arthur replied that I had a special method of tenderising it, no doubt an English standard! I was treated to another wink and had to dash for cover for fear of bursting into giggles.

What a cool guy Arthur was.

True to his word, Arthur handed me a cheque for my first month's salary. This of course meant that I should have to find a bank in which to deposit this wonderful sign of my independence. At the first opportunity, I found the nearest bank, Wells Fargo. What wonderful mental pictures that name provoked, and I asked the kind lady at the customer window if I might open an account. She smiled and assured me we could do that right away, reaching for the appropriate form and bank book for me.

"First of all," she said, "I shall need your full name."

I duly trotted out my name, but on reaching my surname, I said, "I'll have to spell it out for you. It's most unusual and you've probably never heard it before." I spelt out clearly the name Thaw, but was taken aback when she roared with laughter.

"Thaw is one of the most infamous names in America," she said. To my amazement, she related the story of Harry Thaw, the famous murderer who had, in a fit of jealousy, shot dead a man named Stanford White, accusing him of having an affair with his wife. The lady in question was Evelyn Nesbit, who had apparently agreed to marry Harry Thaw after years of being romantically pursued by him. Stanford White was an architect who'd been shot on the roof of his famous building, Madison Square Garden in New York City. Harry Thaw appeared to have been rather unstable, but well connected, and this ensured he escaped the death penalty. He shot what he believed to be his wife's lover directly after a performance of their play. Harry came from an extremely wealthy family and many people believed Evelyn Nesbit had eventually married him for financial security.

For several reasons, all this came as a shock to my system. Firstly, my grandfather had been one of several brothers, and he'd always told the tale about one who lived in New York City and had made a fortune. His name was William Thaw, and when I looked further into the story, I discovered Harry Thaw's father was, in fact, William. I was also told that this was a traditional family name and there was always a William in the Thaw family. My father's name was William. There appeared to be several other connecting facts but, of course, all of this might well be mere coincidence. However, it is still a most unusual name and it did make me think ....

THE GREAT FIRE
OF NOVEMBER 1961

I have always been an early riser, and I particularly loved rising early in California. The light was wonderful and the birds were all new to me, and such a delight at that time of day. Hummingbirds and the beautiful blue birds were just two amazing varieties, complete delights. I would firstly go to the door to retrieve the bottles of milk. Yes, in those days they did have door-step deliveries. I loved those dark brown, dimpled-square glass bottles. I would collect them early in the day, before the heat kicked in, of course. Opening the front door, I would be greeted by a crystal-clear blue sky and wonderful coloured flowers, also completely new to me.

I opened the front door one particular morning, totally unprepared for the sight that met my eyes. Instead of the usual clear blue sky, it was pitch dark outside, and a strange acrid smell filled the air. At first I thought I had mistaken the time and woken whilst it was still dark out, but that would not account for the smell. The dark brown sky made it look like the end of the world had arrived. Quickly, I woke Audrey and Arthur, who shot to the door to see for themselves. They instantly knew it meant a canyon fire.

Neighbours began to assemble in the street, discussing the possibility of evacuating. We switched on the television and saw the news about a raging fire headed straight towards us, racing down the canyons at great speed.

"We should probably be okay," Audrey said. "There's the Freeway between the fire and us, so it can't cross such a wide highway." No sooner had she said this than a gigantic flame leapt across the full width of the eight-lane freeway. It ignited the land on the other side, tearing up the slope at lightning speed, and placing us in the direct line of fire, in every sense of the word.

Moments later, police cars with loud hailers appeared in the street, telling us to take basic needs and evacuate at once. The street was suddenly filled with families packing their cars with children and dogs, preparing to leave. Despite this dire situation, Audrey and I had to laugh, because the lady opposite us was trying to get expensive paintings and furs into the car, ignoring the children crying with fear in the back seat. Suddenly, she let out a blood-curdling scream. It appeared one of her children had vomited on the seat of her brand-new Cadillac.

We packed a small bag for the children, trying to decide where we might go. At this point, there was such a rush to get away from the affected area, and motels were obviously filling up fast. With tongue in cheek, the newspapers reported the following day how sorry they'd felt for the refugees in the Beverly Hilton Hotel.

"Collect your essentials quickly," Audrey said, and I grabbed my passport and trench coat. This caused her great amusement. "It's a fire, not a flood," she said, laughing.

Yes, but my trench coat was indeed my pride and joy, considered high fashion at the time of my departure from England, and I had saved up to buy it. Apart from that, I felt like the bee's-knees wearing it and was not about to leave it behind. To this day, I am still teased about my choice of essentials!

What an experience it proved to be. We drove to Audrey's sister's house and stood on a hill overlooking the fire. It was a sight I shall never forget. The flames roared across the canyon towards Santa Monica and the sea, hundreds of homes lost in its path. Our house was spared. If we had been higher up the canyon road, it would not have stood a chance. So many people were left homeless, including many Hollywood stars. The following morning showed a picture of Kim Novak in the newspaper, hosing down her house with water and great presence of mind.

Whilst Audrey, the children and myself drove away, Arthur refused to budge. We later learned that he and a neighbour had sat it out, playing chess amid all the chaos. It was declared the worst fire in Los Angeles history. Below is a summary of a report from the Los Angeles Fire Department Archives.

SUMMARY:

During the week of November 6, 1961, the city of Los Angeles was visited by the most disastrous brush fire in the history of Southern California. Lashing out from a point of origin high on the north slope of the Santa Monica Mountains, the fire raced through tinder-dry vegetation to the summit, leaped across Mulholland Drive and raged down the south slope into Stone Canyon on a rapidly widening front. Driven savagely before fifty-mile-per-hour winds, the flames sped on south and westward. The canyons and ridges of the coastal slope became engulfed in a veritable hurricane of fire. Thermal air currents, created by the intense heat, coupled with the high velocity winds swirled countless thousands of burning brands aloft to deposit them far in advance of the main fire front. Natural and manmade barriers were utterly incapable of interrupting the progress of the fire under such adverse conditions. Before the wild rush of this roaring destruction was finally subdued, 6,090 acres of valuable watershed had been c consumed. Infinitely more tragic was the incineration of 484 costly residences and 21 other buildings.

Oh, and by the way, did I mention the earthquake? One of the strangest things to adjust to in Los Angeles life was the frequent earth tremors. It was rather unnerving listening to the whole household contents rattling and shaking. From time to time there would be an earthquake large enough on the Richter scale to be worthy of news reporting. At this point, I had not yet experienced one of those, just the low-key variety, which I found worrying enough.

One early summer's night, after I tucked the boys up in bed, I took my book into the lounge for a quiet read. Audrey and Arthur were on a trip for a few days and I was happy to have the two boys alone for a short time. Later in the evening, I went to bed, having checked on the boys and found them sleeping peacefully. It had been a long day and I fell instantly into a deep sleep. The telephone's insistent ringing woke me, and I gazed rather groggily at the bedside clock, shocked to see it was only two A.M. Alarmed, I shot out of bed to answer the telephone, decidedly surprised to hear the voice of the boys' paternal grandmother. This was Grandma Eva, a quiet, sweet lady, and I could not imagine why she would be ringing so early in the morning.

After apologising profusely for waking me, Grandma Eva explained that she could not sleep for thinking about

Jonathan's fish tank. This left me feeling even more confused, until she explained that 'said tank' had been placed on a shelf behind Jonathan's bed and she worried there might be an earthquake, causing the tank to fall directly onto Jonathan's head. True, it was a rather large, square tank, but I put this down to an over-anxious grandma, and believed the chances of the tank actually falling were a little far-fetched. Nevertheless, I promised her that I would go immediately and remove the tank to a safer place. The relief in her voice was palpable. I did exactly that, placing the fish tank on a table in the lounge, and then staggered back to bed. I have to tell you, dear reader, that no more than five minutes later we experienced an earthquake. It caused many things to crash down onto Jonathan's bed, books and toys, etcetera. But thanks to the love of his grandma, not the fish tank!

SURF'S UP!

There is a widely-held belief that when you are about to die your entire life flashes before your eyes. I have to say, it didn't hold true in my case. However, at this particular point in my life, I had not yet lived a great deal, and so perhaps that's why nothing flashed past. I do assure you though, on that day, I was indeed about to die.

It was a beautiful sunny day in Malibu, California, with a crowd of people watching my fate unfold. I was, it should be said, not a beach person. In fact, I loathed a hot beach full of bathers lying with their cheeks in the sand, sticky with sunblock, and turning like chickens on a spit. My idea of enjoying the beach, especially in California, was to visit at night. Living so far south, the sun goes down fairly early, and by eight P.M. it would be fully dark outside.

I found the beach a wonderful experience once the crowds were gone, and the water so tepid it was not unlike swimming in a warm bathtub. With the stars twinkling above, it was sheer perfection. However, submitting to peer pressure one day, I found myself with a car full of friends heading for Malibu in the baking heat, and dreading the adventure. It was, I must admit, a beautiful location.

I quickly realised that to make this day tolerable I should head for the water, where at least I could avoid the worst of the crowds and the heat. Wading out, I passed surfers on their way in. Soon, I broke through the surf line—where the surf breaks and the water is calm, waiting for the next big wave. How I enjoyed the swim, sheer bliss rising and falling with the oncoming waves, until eventually I began to feel rather tired and thought it was time I headed back to the beach. This, I soon learned, was not as easy as it sounded.

I had no idea the proper way to break through the rolling waves as they broke in a line beyond the beach. Eventually, I went straight into them, shocked to find myself thrust towards the bottom by waves so powerful that I could not fight it. I rose to the surface and gasped for air only to be forced down again by the next wave. It was like being in a washing machine with no possible means of exit. Round and round I went from the surface to bottom with scarcely enough time to gasp a mouthful of air between these death rolls. In vain, I tried to wave at my friends sitting on the crowded beach, but they were obviously unaware of my predicament.

As thoughts of what the afterlife might be like filled my head, I tried unsuccessfully not to panic, but my lungs were hurting so much at this point that I thought death would be merciful. Suddenly, to my amazement, I felt a strong pair of hands grab my arms firmly, and in a trice, it seems, I was back on the beach. Apparently, Val eventually realised I was struggling and called the life guard, who had just noticed my predicament and was about to dive in and rescue me.

Exhausted, but relieved, I listened as the lifeguard explained that I should have swum parallel to the waves. This sideways motion would have helped me reach the beach safely. It wouldn't matter, because under no circumstances would I ever enter the blue water of the Pacific again. Indeed, to this very day, I have never ventured into any sea.

Shortly after this life-changing experience, our little group found itself incorporating a couple more members. These two ladies had discovered us through Leah, who worked in the same avenue. Their story was sad but fascinating, though it thankfully had a happy ending after years of abuse. Vivien, the mother, looked to be in her late forties, and her daughter, Sandra, about twenty-one. Sandra, mature for her age, was rather quiet, although not actually shy. We were given the impression that both these very nice ladies were in fact guarded.

As the weeks flew by we gradually began to learn more about this mother-daughter pair. They hailed from Tyneside and spoke with a lovely Geordie lilt. One day over lunch in pretty seaside café, Vivien finally began to thaw and opened up about her story. Sandra's father had been a sullen, cold man, and Sandra confessed to being very scared of him while growing up. She hadn't realized he was an alcoholic until her early teens, a condition that was becoming worse with each passing month. His inevitable loss of temper resulted in him hitting Vivien. Several times these beatings were so severe that hospital treatment was required. Vivien refused to report these events to the authorities, believing it would only cause the violence to escalate. She felt trapped and isolated.

One day the inevitable happened and this violent man attacked Sandra, beating her with considerable force. It turned out this was the straw that broke Vivien's back. She knew they needed to get away from that man, and quickly. At the first opportunity, they packed minimal belongings and fled to a friend's house, hoping for time to consider their next move. All too soon he found them, threatening them from her friend's doorstep. It became clear that this angry man would track them down wherever they went.

And that's exactly what transpired, the two always struggling to stay one step ahead of him. They even tried to move to the South of England once, but he would inevitably find some way to track them down. Unwilling to involve her elderly mother, a frail woman, Vivien decided their only option was to keep running. Something drastic would need to be done.

One day in London, whist riding on a bus, Vivien saw an advertisement for an agency offering employment abroad—a light bulb moment for Vivien. She swiftly left the bus and found the agency. She figured her only hope of escaping their dreadful situation was to flee the country, get as far away as she possibly could. Passports were swiftly acquired, quite possible in those days, and visas arranged. Before they could give the project a second thought, they were on their way. In her bid to protect everyone, Vivian told no one where they were going, not even friends or family. They had secured employment as a nanny and cook-housekeeper for a wealthy businessman. For the first time in years they felt safe, settled and happy in California, but it took a long time for them to feel secure again.

Ultimately, this story had a wonderfully happy ending. Years later, I heard from Vivien that her violent husband had died from a heart attack without ever learning of their location. Sandra, a very attractive young lady, met a young man who turned out to be the son of her employer's business partner, and very wealthy. When Sandra married him, it meant not only happiness, but security for this lovely daughter and her mother. I hope they are still in California and blissfully happy.

NOW WE ARE THREE

I had often told myself that I disliked babies, but to be honest, I had never had much contact with one of those little pink creatures. As an only child, there had not been younger siblings to help take care of, and my job in a medical research laboratory had ill prepared me for children, never mind babies. When Audrey announced that in the coming months there would be a brand-new addition to the family, I found myself less than enthusiastic. As their au pair, I found the two boys simply delightful. I enjoyed playing with them, bathing and reading bed-time stories. But a baby, what on earth would I do with that?

One day I told Audrey that I disliked babies and would be useless at looking after one.

"Not to worry," she told me with a grin. "We shall have a nurse to help at first, and then I shall take over. You get to concentrate on the boys."

Well, I thought that all sounded fair enough and I began to relax, scarcely thinking about the impending new arrival. The day finally dawned and Arthur was about to drive Audrey to the hospital. After giving last minute instruction regarding the children, off they went, Audrey looking amazingly cheerful considering what was about to transpire. Several hours later I got a phone call from a rather groggy Audrey saying they had another little boy, and then she proceeded to tell me about the celebrities they had seen on their way to the hospital. Still star-struck in those days, an amused Audrey would often drive me to places she knew we would see the stars. Bless her, even when about to give birth, she thought I should hear about them.

The new baby did not make a good entrance when he arrived home. Daniel, his two-and-a-half-year-old brother, scowled, declaring the baby was wearing his hat! Daniel was particularly fond of his yellow hat, and the baby was wearing a yellow hat.

One down and three to go.

Jonathan worried the baby might want his books and asked if they could be moved to a higher shelf in his bedroom.

I peeked in at the little red face under the yellow hat and thought all my previous opinions about babies were correct— there was absolutely nothing attractive about them. Thankfully, the nurse arrived and the little party went off to the nursery. The boys and I exchanged knowing looks as we got on with lunch.

Behind the house, at the end of the garden, the ground rose steeply forming a rather vertiginous hill. Audrey had been reluctant to climb this, especially while pregnant. However, the boys and I loved to climb the steep slope via steps made from tree rounds cut into the hill. Upon reaching the top you found the most spectacular view. Isolated from the world below, we would take books, or crayons and paper, and sit happily and peaceful at the top. Snow-covered mountains sat across from us in the distance. This would be my refuge when the baby's presence became intolerable.

Weeks passed and this new arrival did not appear to have any impact on my life, and I was thrilled. One day, however, when Robbie (his new name) was six weeks old, the nurse packed her bags and left. Audrey took over and all was well until one Saturday night not long after the nurse had departed.

Audrey and Arthur announced that they had been invited to an important function and so I would be required to give the baby his evening feed and put him to bed.

I was horrified: taking care of babies was not in my agenda. I declared that I could not possibly undertake such a task. Audrey smiled, then patiently showed me how to give the baby his bottle, burp him and then put him in the cot for a sleep.

Later that evening, the two boys already asleep in bed, I was handed little Robbie and told all would be well, and off they went. I recall shaking with fright as I held the little mite, then popped the bottle into his tiny mouth. To my astonishment, he eagerly started to drink. A tiny hand took hold of mine, little fingers curled around one of mine. I stared down at his rosy cheeks and I had to admit it was a very beautiful sight. After he took his fill, I patted his back, thrilled at the loud burps he made. And then, much to my surprise, he smiled at me. I found tears rolling down my face.

At this point, Audrey put her head around the door, (they had quietly waited to see how I managed) and she said with a grin, "Who does not like babies?" From that moment on I was captivated, and absolutely adored our latest addition to the family.

Several months after Robbie's arrival, Audrey and Arthur were delighted to open an invitation to a very prestigious dinner. It would be the perfect excuse for a new dress to cheer Audrey, not having socialised a lot since the birth of her third son. We had a rather lovely upmarket store close by called *Bullocks of Westwood* and the dress department was a wonder to behold. Sometime earlier, we'd visited Rodeo Drive, but I preferred this lovely large store.

It was decided one morning, after we delivered the two youngest boys to the nursery, that I would accompany Audrey on her shopping expedition to find a new evening dress. I could carry Robbie and give fashion advice—for which I was suitably qualified. So off we went, always a good idea to get input when choosing a new gown. The store was wonderful, cool and stylish, and boasted very interesting clientele.

Sometime later, after trying on several lovely dresses, Audrey made a choice, and indeed she looked wonderful in it, tall and elegant with no hint of a baby bulge. She had started to play tennis again and was toned and fit. She told me she loved tennis. Indeed, I had no idea that tennis was such a big deal, until one day she explained that her partner was Barbra Streisand, a woman she considered witty and funny.

At this point, Audrey left me with the baby to arrange payment for the dress. The baby gazed about with wide-eyed wonder whilst I strolled around the store. I was rather oblivious to other people as I gazed at the stock, when suddenly I found myself bumping into a young man. I hastily apologised and he smiled.

"What is your baby's name?" he asked.

Laughing, I told him, "Robbie, but he isn't mine. I'm an au pair from England."

He may have just been a very polite young man, but he chatted away, asking me if I was enjoying my time in L.A. A little while later, Audrey appeared with her purchase and I said goodbye to the nice man and asked Audrey if she was ready to return home.

She nodded and chuckled before saying, "Have you any idea who you were chatting with?" I told her I didn't. "That was Jonny Mathis."

Bless him, he must have wondered what had hit him!

I was, it had to be said, getting a little blasé about stars at this point. Often when taking Robbie for a walk, the *Tour the Stars' Homes* bus would drive down the avenue and people would stare though the windows, wondering which star had let me push their precious baby out for all to see. I used to smile knowingly and leave them guessing. The house opposite ours was, in fact, the home of Gregory Peck and his wife Veronique, whilst James Garner lived a few doors away. There were more stars than you could shake a magic wand at. Many years later, of course, the O.J. Simpson saga took place at the end of the avenue, and Audrey and Arthur were inundated by rubber-neckers.

Robbie grew and was a delightful child, full of smiles and laughter. Not surprising considering his brothers kept him amused most of the time. We would play a family game of charades on most evenings after dinner. This would take the form of acting out an animal while the rest of the family tried to guess which one. After a while this became almost hysterical, due to Danny's involvement. Jonathan, being the eldest, would act out his animal first and we would all guess, shouting out "tiger" or "elephant" until we guessed correctly. Of course, I had to join in, leaving any chores to wait until the game was complete.

Eventually, it would be Danny's turn, and he would wiggle on the floor while we asked, "Is it a snake?" only to be answered with a loud, "No!" On and on would go the guessing: crocodile, worm, etcetera, and again he replied with a loud, "No!" Eventually we would give in and he would gleefully announce, "It was a fish!" All quite reasonable, you might think, until I explain that every night, and whatever the mime, his answer would always be a fish!

No matter how long we played this game, or how frequently, it always made us laugh hysterically whilst waiting for the fish!

Audrey discovered that not far from our home an enterprising young lady held classes for pre-school children two days a week. The title of these mornings happened to be

Music and Movement, something Audrey thought every little boy should experience. The following week, off they went for an hour of this beneficial activity. On their arrival home, I could see by Audrey's face that this had not exactly been a success. The boys had refused to join in and no amount of persuasion made any difference. This clearly frustrated Audrey, especially as every other child appeared to not only cooperate, but thoroughly enjoyed the experience. "You must take them next time," she announced. "Perhaps they'll join in if you watch."

The morning dawned and we set off full of apprehension, both boys declaring they did not want to go. It was a light, pleasant room and the young lady appeared charming, if a little over enthusiastic. The music began and she announced that the children had to attempt to portray the actions of a window cleaner. Jonathan and Danny pulled a face and shook their heads, refusing to move from the bench. The young lady implored them to reconsider, and suddenly Danny had a bright idea. "I'll dance if Glennyce will," he declared. Or rather, 'Nennis', as he preferred to call me. Jonathan's face lit up, as clearly, he too thought it was a wonderful idea.

"I'm sure she would love to join in," the bright young thing said, and that is how I came to be a window cleaner, a waving tree, an elephant, and countless other wonderful things twice a week with a classful of children under five.

THANKSGIVING

A new and very lovely celebration for me was the festival of Thanksgiving. The boys took part in a play at their nursery school and went off to school dressed as Pilgrims. A family meal had been prepared and it was, I thought, just a practice for Christmas dinner. At least that was how it seemed to me. Turkey and all the trimmings, and pumpkin pie for dessert. My goodness, what a revelation that was, and how I loved that pie.

My Los Angeles family had a dinner for sixteen to prepare, grandparents, aunts, cousins, etcetera, all very exciting and enjoyable. I was never treated as hired help, always as a family member, and I'd been invited to join in the celebratory meal, a lovely experience in every way. There was to be another big celebration that day, and this time Val was giving a very personal thanksgiving for finding Mr Right and getting engaged. August had come into our lives some months earlier and they had instantly fallen in love.

Val was nervous and excited because this was the day she would meet her new family to be. After spending the day with August's family, she would, however, need to be home at some point to help prepare the Thanksgiving dinner set for her employers later in the evening. Audrey and Arthur celebrated their meal at lunch time and so they very kindly told me I could have the evening off. Val's house was just a short walk from mine, and so off I went around five P.M. to watch Val prepare the delicious meal.

The children of Val's family were all teenagers and fairly independent, so her duties mainly consisted of cooking, and a wonderful chef she was. The family would line up each evening to see what type of delightful meal she had produced for them. However, this Thanksgiving evening would be very different. Their extended family had been invited, all of them expecting a spectacular spread. Imagine my surprise on arrival to find no trace of Val. The dining room table had been set but the kitchen was empty. Perhaps even more disturbingly, not a whiff of cooking in the air!

Where on earth had she gone? I had no idea, but felt a sudden surge of relief when August's car pulled into the drive. The kitchen door swung open and Val literally fell inside, drunk as a skunk. She couldn't stand without help, so how on earth could she manage to cook a full dinner? I stared at Val, not sure what to do. Should I try to find her employer and tell them she was ill and unable to cook for them?

"Grief, no," Val said. "I'd be sacked on the spot." I learned she had visited all of August's relatives, one after the other, and been plied with wine and champagne at every stop. Nervous and anxious to please, she had downed the lot, hence the legless state. "Prop me up on the stool," she said. "I shall tell you what to do!"

There followed the most frantic few hours of my life but, under her instruction, I managed to get the turkey in the oven and pressed on with the vegetables. Thank goodness the pumpkin pie had been made the previous evening.

Val found all this hilarious and every time she had a fit of the giggles, I had to prop her back up against the kitchen units (just in case she fell off the high stool)! I began to realise what an adventurous chef Val was, the combination of ingredients totally unknown to me. I was instructed to pour a can of Pineapples into the sweet potatoes. When I questioned her, she assured me, between fits of giggles, that it was indeed what she wanted. We added totally unknown spices (at least to me) to the roast potatoes, and then the weirdest of ingredients to the gravy and sauce—both tasting unlike anything I had ever encountered before—but Val was the boss.

Eventually, when all was almost ready, we heard the cars arriving for the evening feast. At this point, Val was all but asleep, so I quickly hoisted her off the stool and manhandled her to her room, which was mercifully on the ground floor. I threw her mostly on to the bed, where she fell instantly to sleep, then rushed back to the kitchen.

The lady of the house appeared and I told her, "Poor Val has a dreadful migraine, but she managed to cook the dinner before staggering to bed. If you like, I would be happy to stay and serve."

Well, this lovely lady thanked me profusely saying she and her daughter would also help serve. So there you have it, the potential disaster of the year avoided, and all went swimmingly. Early the next morning, I hurried to Val's house to find her nursing a sore head and scarcely able to recall any of the events of the previous evening. I told her about everything and about how all the unusual combinations of food and spices had been so very new to me.

"What combinations?" she asked. I told her what I had added to the food and her eyes almost popped out on stalks.

It seems she had been clutching ideas from the air, far too drunk and clueless to know what she was saying. None of the combinations made any sense. At this point the good lady of the house appeared, thanking me once more for helping out. She told Val the meal had been a huge success, everyone so surprised and delighted at the unusual flavourings and food combinations. They assumed it must have been an English-inspired meal.

"Why, yes," Val agreed. "So glad you like it."

We laughed fit to burst once she left, but eventually Val said, "Glenn, I owe you big time."

"You better believe it," I replied, but then again, she had saved my life, so it did seem only fair to repay the gesture!

REVELATIONS

Well, as I have mentioned before, I found California amazingly colourful in every way, especially after arriving from a post-war Britain. People dressed in brightly-patterned clothes walked among white and pastel-coloured buildings, but it was the multi-coloured shoes that proved to be most mind -blowing to us.

We discovered fairly early in our sojourn a wonderful store named Orbach's on Wilshire Boulevard. The shoe department in this store rendered us speechless and full of wonder. At that time, the U.K. could provide black, brown, white and, occasionally, red shoes. Orbach's produced an entire floor of shoes in colours we could only have dreamt about: lilacs, apricots, yellows, blues and pinks. We stared open-mouthed at the variety, feeling as if we had been living in a black and white film that suddenly turned to colour.

Another, and very important, aspect of the abundance we encountered in California was the food. We were introduced to pizza for the first time. How amazing was that! And we also discovered the wonderful Mexican food, freely available in our areas, and Chinese food. Perhaps the most enjoyable of all, at least for me, was discovering Will Wright's Ice Cream Parlour. This palace of delight, with its candy-striped interior, high stools and glass tables, produced a menu of mouth-watering delights. There were so many varieties of ice cream that it was virtually impossible to make a choice. Toppings for these delights left one bewildered, though the finished article tended to be a thing of art and beauty.

Sooner or later this abundance would, of course, take its toll and one day Val moaned to me that she was piling on the pounds. "Me too," was all I could say. We realised then that something would have to be done to curb this enthusiasm for newly discovered goodies.

On our next day off, Val announced that she had found the perfect slimming diet in a magazine she'd bought. "Here's the thing," she said, "we get to eat nothing but melon."

Well, it was true that we both loved melon, and living in Los Angeles we could find varieties never seen or heard of before, but just eating melon felt a little drastic. At that point, Val was determined, and we decided that the following day we would visit the wonderful Farmers' Market at Westwood to buy the melons.

Full of bewitching sights and sounds, the market was a fun place to spend time. To Val's delight, there were melons of every variety and size, and all were extremely inexpensive. This was going to be the diet for her, no doubt about it, and so at the end of the afternoon we went to purchase said melons. The larger the melon, the cheaper the price, and so with great enthusiasm Val chose a huge green watermelon. We were told that beast weighed twelve pounds and Val said it would last her several days, by which time she hoped to have lost the same amount of weight. Reality hit right after paying the lady. Scarcely able to lift the beast and we had to take it home on the bus. Between fits of giggles, each of us took one end of the mammoth melon and we staggered amid onlookers to the nearest bus stop.

It took a huge effort to carry it on the bus, and to this day I can recall what the bus driver said, though I can't bring myself to repeat it! Staggering from the bus in the heat, we finally arrived at Val's house, but then we realised it would have to be cut into pieces to stay fresh, or indeed to fit into the refrigerator. Even though her kitchen contained an enormous fridge it was soon full to bursting with melon slices. When her employers saw the contents of their fridge, they clearly thought the heat had finally melted her brain. Several days later, I checked with Val on how her melon diet was going.

"Don't talk to me about bloody melon," she said. "I am sick of the sight of it!"

The summer of 1962 was shaping up to be very hot—and, perhaps, the novelty of blue skies every day was beginning to wear off. Oddly, I found myself wishing for it to rain. The day it finally did proved to be chaotic for the locals. It was the first rainfall in two years, a heavy downpour that proved to induce sheer panic. Teenagers driving around in old convertible cars with surf boards poking out of the back seat suddenly found themselves soaking wet. They had no idea how to put up the top and, even if they did, the tops were often rusted into the folded position. Windscreen wipers also failed for many, and mud covered everything.

Despite the chaos, we Brits enjoyed the day immensely. It was an eventful summer for many reasons, and one day in particular remained etched in my memory. The street where I lived was in the beautiful, leafy suburb of Brentwood with many wonderful houses of all shapes and designs. However, I was intrigued to learn that the most modest of those houses, a bungalow farther down the street from my home, belonged to Marilyn Monroe. How I longed to catch a glimpse of this hugely popular and controversial figure, though sadly, no matter how many times we drove up and down the street to reach Sunset Boulevard, I never did see the star.

Early in August, the 8th to be precise, we woke to a commotion of sirens. Police cars and vans of every description raced up and down from Sunset Boulevard before the street was sealed off to everyone, including residents.

When the commotion finally receded, we discovered the awful truth about why there had been such a large police, and other official groups, presence.

Marilyn Monroe had been found dead in our usually quiet neighbourhood! We could scarcely believe it and, of course, it gave rise to such a media circus and scrum for ages afterwards. The street became a magnet for every newspaper and television journalist in Los Angeles. Indeed, it was very strange to feel that on our very doorstep, as it were, such a sad event of worldwide interest had occurred.

Having been resident in Los Angeles for some time now, the au pair girls had ventured forth to many areas of this enormous city. We began to feel like we should perhaps take a look further afield. Val fancied a visit to Palm Springs, which did indeed sound romantic, not to mention exotic. We discovered that we could take one of the long-distance bus routes all the way, anticipating our first experience travelling through the Mojave Desert.

It proved to be a fascinating little town, and extremely wealthy inhabitants spawned streets filled with expensive shops. On the outskirts of town, yet another world, the rich and famous owned ranches and golf courses. After a long, exciting day, we headed back to the bus for the long ride back to Los Angeles. Climbing aboard, we realised we would not be able to sit together, as there appeared to be only the odd seat vacant throughout the bus. Val had to sit at the very back and I took a seat at the very front. The usual routine was to drive to a central point in the desert to refuel the bus, and indeed the passengers, but this only happened during the daytime. Late at night the bus merely stopped to transfer passengers headed for another destination.

Her expression stern, Val warned me to concentrate. "Don't get off at the change-over stop."

"I won't."

It was hot and very late when we pulled into the change-over stop and I woke from a deep sleep as the door swung open and the driver shouted, "All change."

Following several passengers, I jumped up and stepped off the bus into a scene of organised madness. Buses were screeching to a halt in all directions and people were scrambling on and off as drivers shouted, "San Diego" or "Santa Barbara." There was an ant-like scurrying as people jumped aboard with lightning reflexes, and the drivers took off again.

It took only a minute or two for me to realise the pickle I was in. My bus, bound for Los Angeles, had departed along with all the others into the stygian darkness of the desert night. Stunned, I found myself alone, Val's words suddenly ringing in my ears. 'Do not get off at the change-over stop!'

Too late. I had been half asleep and following people like a dazed sheep out into the night. Once my plight finally dawned on me, I started to panic, wondering what on earth I should do. It was two A.M. and I was stuck in the middle of a cold desert night.

Suddenly, in the distance, I saw lights approaching from the road, a bus driving at great speed into the square. It halted and the door swung open and a rage-filled face popped out, a voice shouting a north of England expression, "Oi, dozy kipper, get in here!" Val had realised what I'd done, the very thing she told me not to, and persuaded the bus driver to turn around to retrieve me. To this day, when she is mad at me, my nickname is 'Dozy Kipper'.

LAST OF THE BIG SPENDERS

Having ventured as far as Palm Springs, our appetite for further exploring was whetted and we decided to visit Las Vegas. My goodness that sounded glamorous and adventurous. In those days, I knew of no one who had visited this city of fun. In fact, it is true to say I knew no one in England who had visited the U.S.A. We would drive all the way, four of us going on this adventure. One of our people had in fact been provided with a car for her job. How exciting! Audrey, who was a little concerned, warned us to take plenty of bottled water for this long, lonely desert road. In those days, there were few places to stop.

At last the arrangements were made and we piled into the car full of beans and anticipation. The plan was to spend the weekend there—find a reasonable hotel where we might stay and perhaps take in a show. We had packed cool wear for the day and a decent dress for evenings. All would be perfect.

My goodness it was hot, but the Mojave Desert at close quarters was a sight to behold. It took little imagination to picture all those cowboy movies being filmed there. I had never seen such a long, straight road before, or since. It was with great excitement that we realised this road would eventually come to an end at Las Vegas. The city loomed on the horizon like a hazy mirage in the desert. Before we knew it, we were driving down the main street filled with all the sights and sounds we had previously only seen on film, the whole scene surreal.

After parking the car, we decided to explore before finding a small hotel for the night. Exploring was hot dusty work and we soon gave up in favour of a snack and a long cold drink. We realised, with something of a shock to our system, that this was an expensive town. The snack and drink had cost a small fortune and suddenly it began to dawn on us that we might be unable to afford a motel.

This proved to be the case and there followed a bizarre few days of washing in public bathrooms and sleeping in the car. The posh frocks never came out of the case, just as the glamorous shows on the Strip went unseen. We arrived home impoverished and decidedly grubby, though definitely the wiser!

The next foray into the wider world was to be a quick trip to Mexico. Not far down the coast of southern California, we would be able to drive through the lovely city of San Diego before crossing the border into Tijuana. Day trips across the border were all the rage in those days. We had been advised that the best way to enter Mexico was through a tourist bus north of the border. Park the car and spend the day exploring this busy town.

All went smoothly, and we explored San Diego on the way. With its strong Spanish influence, each of us found this city beautiful. We were excited to find a large Mexican quarter with wonderful shops and cafés full of music (our expectation of Mexico) just a short drive away. We knew that all the places along the coast of California had a strong Spanish influence—due to pilgrims travelling this way from across the border—and it seemed that wherever they stopped to rest they had founded missions with religious names. San Diego, Los Angeles, Santa Monica, Santa Barbara, and many more beautiful missions were to be found along this coast—like the wonderful San Juan Capistrano, home of the legendary swallows. (They returned on the same day at the exact same time each year.)

Well, here we were, about to enter Mexico for the first time, and jolly excited we were. After parking the car, we boarded the bus to cross the border, all fairly straightforward after displaying our passports. Alighting in the centre of Tijuana, we were instantly accosted by men leading donkey carts. They tried to persuade us to climb aboard to have our pictures taken in sombreros. Of course, being silly tourists, we found ourselves with ridicules pictures of grinning idiots in sombreros bearing the names 'Rosita and Bonita'—plus quotes that must have been the equivalent of 'kiss me quick' etcetera. It really felt like Blackpool in the heat!

We'd been told that a 'must see' was the bull ring and, as none of us had ever seen one, we asked how we might find it. We were advised to go by local bus, (found in the corner of this main square). It would take us directly to the arena and it would drop us off right outside the magnificent building. We climbed aboard, asking for the bullring.

"*Si, si*," we were assured, and off we went. With few seats, the bus turned out to be quite an experience, most people sitting on the floor, along with their children, dogs and chickens. Lurching at a dangerous angle, we sped along until eventually we were informed that the bull ring was right ahead.

The bull ring was indeed well worth seeing, but I was eternally grateful there was not a fight taking place during our visit. I hated the thought of bull fights with a passion. However, we did get to look around this huge building in the baking heat. Though impressed, I was also happy when the time came to catch the bus back to the square. The bus lurched into view and we asked in our best Spanish if this was going to the main square. Assured once more that it was, we climbed aboard.

The route this time appeared to take longer than on arrival and we started to worry a little that we might not be headed back to the main square. Suddenly the square came into view and we heaved a sigh of relief, anxious to depart this lurching vehicle. Much to our dismay the bus shot through the square at great speed. Before we could shout stop, we ended up at the top of the next hill on the other side. Frustrated, we could see the large tourist bus waiting in the square to take us back to the border.

We felt our spirits lift as the square finally came into view again, but were thwarted again as the bus shot up yet another hill in the opposite direction. It would be a disaster if our homeward-bound bus left for the last trip back to the U.S. without us. At last the elusive square came into view for the third time and, feeling desperate, we all lunged at the driver, yelling at him to stop. In somewhat of a shocked state, we finally exited the small bus, climbing aboard our main bus, and were informed we had made it with a couple of minutes to spare! Looking back, I could swear I saw the little bus driver laughing, guessing that tourists were likely his main source of amusement on hot boring days. I was not sorry to see the back of Mexico on that occasion.

GOING SEPARATE WAYS

It was clear the au pair girl band was about to split up. Members were getting restless for newer pastures, and some were even going home, feeling they had explored enough. However, the first major split was caused by Val, who was about to marry her Mr Right. We could not argue with her decision because he was a lovely man and clearly the love of Val's life.

August, her fiancé, passed the test for me on Christmas Eve, just a short time after the Thanksgiving trauma Val and I had lived through. I had a few concerns about Val making the correct decision. After all, it would be a lifetime in California and she was very English indeed. Suppose it turned out he was not the right man for Val? It would be a disaster.

That Christmas would be a difficult one for me. I missed my family and a traditional English Christmas. My Los Angeles family were of Jewish faith and so did not celebrate Christmas. It felt a little strange not to put up a Christmas tree.

On Christmas Eve, Audrey and Arthur were going to a party at a friend's house and I, of course, was babysitting. I was feeling homesick—parcels from home always took longer than people realized and hadn't yet arrived. With Val and August planning an outing, it felt a little bleak. Suddenly there was a knock at the door. Perplexed, I swiftly rose to answer, wondering who on earth would be calling on

Christmas Eve. August stood outside with a gift in his hand for me.

Smiling, he said, "I thought you might be feeling a little homesick. I wanted you to have at least one gift to let you know someone was thinking about you."

I thanked him profusely, and when he had gone I opened the parcel to find a record of Dave Brubeck playing my favourite piece of his. Earlier in the year, Val, August and myself had been to a Dave Brubeck concert at the University of Los Angeles, where August had studied. He knew how much I loved the music, and especially that particular piece. At that moment, in my mind, he was one of the kindest and most thoughtful people I had ever met. I felt one hundred percent certain that Val was indeed marrying the right man. He would look after her, and she would be extremely happy.

Incidentally, one of the great joys of living in Los Angeles (at that moment in time) was the great music scene. It's true to say I attended many fantastic concerts at the legendary *Free Trade Hall* in Manchester. Famous stars such as Ella Fitzgerald, Dizzy Gillespie, Count Basie, and even my favourite Dave Brubeck, all appeared, though we had to wait ages at times for these great musicians to visit. Musical stars abounded and we had wonderful concerts to attend on a regular basis. I particularly loved Shelly Manne, and was delighted to be around when he opened the *Shelly Manne Hole* in Hollywood. I had visited jazz clubs during my teens in Manchester, listening to the wonders of Aker Bilk and Monty Sunshine, whist equally enjoying the visit to the Free Trade Hall of the Modern Jazz Quartet. Oddly enough, I loved both traditional and modern jazz. Most of my friends appeared to be fanatical about one style of jazz over the other, but for me it was all superb. But I digress ....

We would, each of us au pair pals, be bridesmaids at the wedding. After the big day, Val and August would move to an apartment in another part of Los Angeles. The wedding day was alternatively funny and tearful, emotional because it was Val's birthday and all her family was still at home in England.

I rode in the car with Val, who had in tribute to her homeland worn a dress of Tudor elegance. It had long sleeves and a full skirt, though the headdress would have to be a pointed Tudor confection draped with pearls and, of course, one large pearl hanging from the central point. Val had made this wonderful headdress herself, the only problem being that with so many other things to arrange, she'd run out of time and the headdress was unfinished. Not at all fazed, Val produced her sewing kit on the way to the church and stitched the remaining pearls in place.

After a lovely wedding, we all arrived back at Val's wonderful employer's home for the poolside reception. How gorgeous it all looked, huge vases of white flowers arranged all around the pool.

Val thanked her employer, in awe that she had bought all those beautiful blooms, but she was left somewhat confused when her employer replied, "No, I thought you had."

The truth eventually dawned. The best man, in all his enthusiasm for duty, had stripped the church of flowers and brought them home, believing them to be Val's. However, it turned out they belonged to the church and the four other weddings about to take place that day! In a panic-fuelled dash, he returned them just in time for the next wedding.

Val married August on her birthday in March, just before Easter that year. Suddenly, stores, gardens and malls were full of giant rabbits. At this point in time, Easter was very low key in England—just the odd chocolate egg and chapel services ruled the day. In Los Angeles, however, huge displays and parades made this a celebratory occasion. I found it easier to cope with this than the Christmas scenes: huge snowmen standing on artificial snow, reindeer romping across hot roofs, and Christmas trees twinkling to the backdrop of a blazing sun and blue skies. I thought, as the famous Tim Vine once said, *'It is like someone breaking wind in an elevator, wrong on so many levels!'* Easter, however, was different, bunnies, flowers and parades blending nicely into the sunshine.

I had at this point gone out on a couple of dates with a rather nice young man and was delighted when he rang to say he was planning a surprise outing for Easter Sunday. He said I was to be up at the crack of dawn to pack a blanket and flask of coffee, and maybe a cookie or two. To say I was intrigued was an understatement, but I eagerly looked forward to the morning.

In the pitch-black of early morning, I waited for my new friend to arrive. Rather bleary-eyed, I tiptoed out of the house in order not to wake everyone, and off we went. I soon realised we were heading for the Hollywood hills, eventually joining a stream of cars heading in the same direction. To my surprise, we arrived at the famous Hollywood Bowl, this wonderful natural amphitheatre filling up with people clutching their blankets around their knees against the early morning chill. It was, my friend revealed, the Easter Sunday sunrise service and I would be in for a surprise. Indeed, I was, for as the sun began to rise over the hills, figures dressed in white and holding golden trumpets appeared at the highest points all around this wonderful theatre. They began to play, heralding the dawn, and it gave one goose bumps!

I experienced even more goose bumps when, only moments later, Charlton Heston came striding across the stage in the sun's early morning light! How appropriate for such an occasion. Looking suitably biblical and very handsome indeed, he gave the opening words and read the first lesson beautifully. Marvellous choirs sang and the whole morning service was moving and quite magical in such a splendid setting. It had certainly been worth getting out of bed in the middle of the night to see!

It felt like the end of an era at this point. Elaine went home to the Scilly Isles and many of the other au pairs either went home or moved on. Val had also moved away and I pondered on what I should do next. I adored my new family, but there was a big world out there and I had barely scratched the surface. Leah, at this precise moment, declared that she had itchy feet and was thinking of moving to San Francisco. It sounded like a very attractive proposition and I immediately decided to join her. Saying a tearful goodbye to the Greenberg family, I assured them I should, in all probability, land once more back in Los Angeles.

Union Station was an exciting place to be when traveling. I was no longer simply sitting on a beautiful leather sofa dreaming of the far-away places the trains might take me. This time I was actually about to leave on one. After we booked our seat, a 'Red Cap' took our luggage and placed it in the right carriage for us. The train had wonderful arched windows vaulting over the whole ceiling giving a panoramic view of the scenery—scenery that left one breathless as the train made its way north, four hundred miles up the Pacific coast to San Francisco. A truly wonderful experience, and the excitement mounted as we pulled into the final station.

We would have to find somewhere to stay that night and then organise ourselves in earnest the following day. The next day we were directed to an advice agency, and rather splendid advice it turned out to be. We were given a list of prospective apartments to rent and told, in no uncertain terms, not to rent south of a certain street. If we managed to find an apartment and settle in, we should return to the agency immediately and they would help us find employment—the nature of which we had no idea, but it all sounded most encouraging.

After visiting a few apartments, we swiftly realised that we would be unable to afford any of them. Despite advice to the contrary, the only apartments we could afford were situated in the district we had been warned against. It was Hobson's choice and eventually we took a clean, if basic, apartment in a large dreary-looking block. Despite the bleakness, it felt exciting to be completely independent and I hurriedly emptied my suitcase, filling the wardrobe and drawers. Leah was much more laid back about it all and said she would make coffee first and then we would go shopping for groceries. On arrival, we had noticed a small store on the corner selling most household items and we decided we would go and buy essentials there.

The shopkeeper was rather dour and we realised he was of Native American descent. It dawned on us that everyone we had seen that afternoon had likewise been of this culture. Taking our brown paper bags full of items, we pondered this fact on the walk back to our apartment, wondering what implications, if any, it might have for us. On entering the flat, we were shocked by the sight that met our eyes. It was a shamble, all my clothes pulled from the wardrobe, scattered all over the room. Clearly not the style they were looking for because none had been taken. But then we discovered that Leah's packed suitcase was gone. Poor dear, she'd lost her clothes, valuables, money and passport. Her heart sank as we wondered what on earth our next move might be.

I suggested we go straight back to the advice centre in the morning and see what we should do next. Leah would leave more than her heart in San Francisco! Exhausted, we sank into the sofa and switched on the television set in the corner of the room in time to view the evening news, totally unprepared for what we saw next. The little grocery store we had visited only an hour before appeared on the screen, the newsreader announcing that the dour shopkeeper had been the victim of a robbery and shot dead!

Welcome to San Francisco.

The following morning, our trusty advice lady said, "Now you know why I told you not to take an apartment in that district." Apparently, and sadly at this point in the history of this lovely city, many North American Indigenous peoples had left their reservations and headed for the big city. They soon discovered that they had a huge alcohol problem and found themselves in ghettos where, fuelled by alcohol and depression, they turned to crime. Leah was put in touch with the British Embassy, who helped with her passport and other necessary items, and we were given interviews for employment. It became obvious fairly quickly that we hadn't thought this move through. This city was a tourist destination and many jobs were, in fact, only seasonal.

We arrived in San Francisco at the beginning of autumn, which proved not to be such a smart move, not many jobs of interest available. But at this point, we simply wanted to keep body and soul together. I was given an interview at a famous restaurant on Fisherman's Wharf, the significance of which I was unaware of initially. I soon learned just how famous this location was and, to my delight, the quickest way of getting there was by cable car. What a wonderful experience that turned out to be, and what a picturesque ride up and down the steep hills until we eventually descended to the wharf.

The job involved boiling shrimp for the evening meals – lots and lots of shrimp. I was glad to be riding home via the cable car, open to the elements and able to disperse the smell of fish from my person. However, the biggest surprise of all about this restaurant turned out to be the owner: Joe Di Maggio, world famous baseball player and the ex-husband of Marilyn Monroe—who, as I sadly reported earlier, had recently died. It felt like a very spooky connection.

As the city emptied of tourists, the shops and cafés became decidedly quieter and we both found our jobs in jeopardy. After only a couple of months we were out job hunting again. The kind, helpful lady at the agency smiled and said she would see what could be found, but to try not to get our hopes up.

Several weeks passed and soon we found it a challenge to pay the rent and bills, and even eating became a challenge. Being a bit of a fruit freak however, I triumphed over adversity by eating peaches, glorious, gigantic, and costing only pennies. I remembered Val and her melon diet as the pounds fell away.

At last the kind lady at the agency came up with the goods. I had an interview at one of the city centre hotels as a desk receptionist, and Leah went along to see if she might have a job at the Greyhound Bus office. To our delight, and not a moment too soon, we both managed to secure employment. Luckily, we lived within walking distance of the hotel and, I kid you not, it was named the *Hotel California*! On reflection, I do wonder if this is the one made famous by the *Eagles* but, of course, I could not be sure.

The hotel was owned by a family, the current owners the third generation to take on this lovely building. The wife in this set-up was rather frail, and I thought fairly old, but as it turned out she was only in her early sixties, recovering from a hysterectomy. She languished on the sofa in their private apartments most of the day wearing a silk dressing gown. Placed strategically by the day bed was always a large scotch, which I thought somewhat added to the glamour. I was told that whenever she contacted the front desk for anything, it was my duty to deliver her requirements. One morning there came a request for a slice of cake from the kitchens and, as instructed, I visited the cook and secured said cake. Delivering it to the lady, I was told to place it on the coffee table, but as my gaze returned to eye level, I had the shock of my life to see this lady totally naked. After slipping off her gown, she informed me that I must inspect her scar, and she told me all about the operation. I was off my food for days!

As we had a fairly decent income at that point, it was decided we could probably move to a new apartment. This would be in a much more pleasant area, and hopefully a little larger than the old one. We found a place overlooking the very lovely Golden Gate Park and enjoyed walking through this leafy spot for fresh air. However, the air gradually became less fresh as time went by, because the park began to fill daily with a group of young people singing—and smoking a peculiar-smelling brand of cigarettes.

Innocents abroad, we had no idea what 'whacky baccy' was, and that what transpired was the very beginning of flower-power and the drop-out generation. Tents began to appear and music would fill the air. It was all rather intriguing and I found myself wondering how they survived (like maybe they too only ate peaches). At that point in time the area remained fairly low key, but in a few short years this would become the famous Haight-Ashbury District and would mushroom into the huge flower-power movement, the summer of love and all that jazz.

This city was shaping up to be a fascinating place for the *beautiful* people to live. It was a city like no other I had ever seen before. The steep streets shot up almost vertically into the air, or veered steeply downhill, so much so that cars tended to park at right angles to the curb instead of alongside. Sky scrapers on top of hills made for wonderful scenery, and the whole city being surrounded by water on three sides offered spectacular sea views from every angle. We grew to love the place, especially wonderful shops like the *City of Paris*. They were marvellous to look around in, but so exclusive that I very much doubt we ever bought anything.

The new apartment was light and bright, and a good deal more spacious than the old cramped one. For all that though, the layout was a little odd. The small entrance hall led into a large sunny lounge and open kitchen. Behind this lounge was a large bathroom, and the only bedroom revealed a single bed.

We found it interesting that in the lounge there was a hidden double bed designed to pull down from the wall. By day it looked like wood panelling, but when a handle was pulled, it flipped down to almost fill the entire lounge area.

Leah desperately wanted the bedroom, and I willingly agreed to let her have it when I bounced on the double bed, the mattress divinely comfortable. There would be no one to see me after all; and so we settled on this arrangement. All went well until one night Leah went out with a group of new friends and uncharacteristically found herself very drunk. It was quite late when I heard the front door open and Leah staggered inside. Imagine my horror when I realised she was not alone. Standing behind her was a tall man wearing an ex-army greatcoat and smiling inanely at me. What a situation; there I was in my pyjamas drinking hot chocolate and reading a book in the middle of the lounge, staring at the drunken twosome!

As they lurched past me into the kitchen, I hastily switched off the bedroom light and snuggled down into bed. Sometime later they appeared again, and this time Leah got under the covers with me. The young man, still wearing his great coat, lay on top. Leah assured me they would be no trouble, but there was far more room in my bed than hers. What a situation: but I was so tired that I found myself falling asleep. When I woke the next morning, to my amazement the young man had gone, never to be seen again.

This city was extremely rich in culture, as Leah was to experience first-hand one fine evening. Many members of Leah's family had connections to the arts, if not actually artists themselves. Her brother-in-law was a famous Shakespearian actor and her cousin an opera singer. Imagine Leah's delight therefore when said cousin contacted her and announced she would be singing with her company at the famous San Francisco Opera House and she would secure a ticket for Leah to attend the performance.

Oh my, what excitement, and what trepidation regarding what she should wear. A long black velvet skirt was purchased to complement a bright peacock-blue top. To this Leah decided to add a black velvet ribbon tied around her hair. She would pin a wonderful diamond brooch in the centre of this ribbon, and wear her grandmother's diamond ring. Thankfully, Leah always carried these objects in her handbag and therefore they'd not been stolen during the break-in of our apartment. I was pressed into styling her hair, not a natural forte of mine, but I did my best. Leah's long fair hair, fine with a slight curl, was to be swept upwards at the ends for a cute chic look, and I think I almost achieved this.

We pinned the diamond brooch to the ribbon, made her makeup heavier than usual, and I had to say the result was quite impressive. I assured her she would look very much at home amongst the opera crowd. Off we went, Leah with a spring in her step in the direction of the opera house. I walked with her to the door, anxious to see the crowds of opera goers arriving. As I have mentioned before, San Francisco is surrounded by water and would often be suddenly engulfed in fog. Most mornings and evenings would see this fog descend rapidly. The night of the opera was no exception and as we walked along, the fog became quite thick. By the time we had arrived at the famous Opera House, Leah's fine English hair had fallen victim to the moist air. She looked like Harpo Marks in drag by the time she walked through the entrance! Bless her, Leah was too excited to even think about her hair and would notice nothing amiss until after the performance.

Weeks later, Leah announced that an actor friend was visiting from England and would be taking her to dinner. I was most impressed; this girl truly did have thespian connections. He rang and arranged to meet her the following evening for a nice long chat. Sometime after this conversation, her friend rang once again to say that he was staying with a fellow actor and, as she obviously had a flat mate, would we like to make up a foursome. I had never in my life had a blind date and the thought filled me with dread. Suppose he expected a willowy blonde, all teeth and tanned like the Pan American hostess? I was short and, even after years in California, disappointingly white.

I shook my head at Leah, but she handed the phone to me anyway, saying the young man in question would like a word with me. Taking a gulp of air, I took the phone with shaking hands. Oh my, what a voice, deep plummy English, and totally charming. This unnerved me even more and, as my confidence plummeted to an all-time low, I searched desperately for an excuse to say no. I found myself blurting out that I was short, bespectacled, overweight and full of spots and was sure to be a disappointing dinner date. (Only two of these facts happened to be true. I leave you to ponder which two!)

He laughed a loud plummy laugh, saying, "Well, actually that is good news, because I too am short of stature, grossly overweight, cursed with a large bald head and bandy legs, so we shall make the perfect couple."

I groaned. It appeared he had a great sense of humour, leaving me no excuse not to go. With sinking heart on the appointed evening, I did the best I could with the material available and tried to look attractive. Leah assured me all would be well and that I looked perfectly acceptable. We arrived first at the designated eating spot, and Leah suddenly declared that her friend was approaching our table. A very tall, handsome man appeared and gave Leah a kiss on the cheek, claiming it was wonderful to see her. I looked beyond for my companion, and lo and behold there he was—short, grossly overweight, with a large bald head and bandy legs! I gave thanks to God that they were only in town for one night.

EMPLOYMENT OPPORTUNITIES GALORE

With the arrival of spring came the return of the tourists and soon the shops and newspapers were filled with adverts for jobs. Leah found a job in a lovely dress shop and became excited at the prospect of a staff discount. I perused the local paper, as my hotel job would be coming to an end shortly, this being a six-month arrangement.

One particular job caught my eye. It promised to teach massage skills to enthusiastic learners. The salon said it specialised in sports injuries and would also teach how to use equipment, such as steam boxes—whatever those were. I thought these might be useful skills to have, especially if I moved on again, and so I applied. The lady on the telephone sounded rather nice and friendly, although I did think some of her questions were a little odd. For instance, was I comfortable with the opposite sex, and did I consider myself attractive. Here we go again, I thought. *Yes, indeed*, I replied, a bit of a lie, but at this point I was interested.

Hopefully looking my best after a good scrub up, I went along for my interview. I was met by a very glamorous lady, wearing what I considered to be far too much makeup, at the salon reception desk. She called for the manager, who appeared through a bead curtain and instructed me to follow her. We entered a large, white-painted room filled with tables and the 'steam boxes'. Several contained men who were, unsurprisingly, steaming.

"Good for the skin," the manager assured me, and then added, "When their time comes to a close in these contraptions, the men will have their massage." She would show me what was required, and then I would show her that I had the necessary talent by attending to the next client.

I began to feel a little uneasy, but watched as she opened the door to the box and instructed the man to lie on the table. He threw away the towel he had been wearing and, with a grin, asked her for 'The Special'.

The execution of the 'special' brought me a hot sweat that would have rivalled those in the sweat box. I swiftly told the manager that I seriously did not think the job was for me. Backing out of the place as fast as my legs would carry me, I ran all the way home to blurt out the story to a much-amused Leah.

I quickly realised my next job was to be by far my favourite whilst living in San Francisco. It was, in fact, as sales assistant at the very busy Woolworths store. How I loved that cheap and cheerful shop, marvelling at the range of goods for sale, everything one needed in daily life, as well as an awful lot one did not need. When I received my wage at the end of each week, I would spend a great deal of time perusing the many counters and then spending a portion of it in the store. All the other members of staff proved to be extremely friendly and good fun. Everything was so very inexpensive that I found myself facing problems with money. Hard to imagine I found a currency of decimalisation more of a problem than pounds, shillings and pence, but I did. Eventually this would, of course, be very helpful when Britain adopted decimalisation, for then I had no trouble at all.

One of my favourite counters in Woolworths happened to be the one selling jewellery. Cheap and garish and I thought so very cheerful. I discovered at that point in my life that this type of embellishment was simply ideal. One week I bought myself a pair of drop-pearl earrings that looked amazingly authentic, and quite classy compared to the rest of the stock available. I enjoyed wearing them. Many years later, when back home in England, I attended a rather 'posh' event and found myself sitting at the table of a dowager festooned with expensive pearls. I, of course, was wearing my Woolworth earrings, hoping no one would compare them to the amazing variety of the real deal on display.

Suddenly a lady asked if my pearls were real and before I could answer the dowager said in a sharp tone of voice, "Of course they are, what a rude question. I can tell quality when I see it."

I beamed beatifically at the dowager and the lady who had asked the question, hoping they could not discern the relief I felt. To this day, I do not know if the dowager was terribly kind or myopic!

To my deep sadness, the job at *Woolworths* also came to an end, everything here purely transitory and seasonal. Once again, I found myself in the hands of the nice lady at the employment bureau. This time the job offered was a complete surprise, as receptionist for a dental practice. Well, I could not complain about the lack of variety!

There was a slight problem in that this dental practice was across the Golden Gate Bridge in a delightful little place called Sausalito. It would involve travelling, but I thought I really should give it a go. Sausalito was extremely pretty, directly opposite San Francisco, and offered a stunning view of that city. I could catch a bus, which thankfully did not take nearly as long as I'd anticipated.

The dentist who interviewed me was an extremely pleasant man, one of only two in the practice. The dental nurses and administration staff all appeared warm and friendly and I gladly accepted the offer of a job as receptionist. It turned out that they liked my English accent and asked me to "lay it on" when answering the telephone. For their approval, I tried to sound more 'Queen's English' and less a Lancashire lass. I was not the only new employee. On the same day I started, there was also a sweet young dental nurse, this being her first job.

The building was a large, wooden house which had once been a family home. The reception desk was on the ground floor, along with treatment rooms and a small lounge for patients to recover if needed. The first floor consisted of a kitchen and rather large and comfortable staff lounge, and a small corridor leading off this lounge for storage.

It was all very casual at lunchtime. We could cook in the kitchen if we wished or eat our packed lunch. Lunch times were staggered, so there were few numbers taking breaks at the same time, though I found everyone very friendly. After a couple of weeks, I settled into a routine, looking forward to each day. One day the newest nurse shared her lunch time with me and whilst we chatted she asked who was the man occupying the room at the end of the storage corridor, wondering if he was to be another dentist.

I was rather perplexed because I had never seen another man in the building other than the two usual dentists. As she prepared to return to her work, the nurse said, "He may not be a dentist because he doesn't wear a white tabard, just a black polo-necked sweater."

I told her that he must be in charge of supplies, maybe a sort of warehouse man. At this point, one of the dentists appeared to eat his lunch and I asked him about the chap down the corridor. He looked uncomfortable, but said he would have a word with the young nurse.

Several days later, some of the staff had gathered in the lounge for lunch when the young nurse asked once again about the man in the office down the corridor. A silence descended in the room and eventually the dentist said, "I'm sorry, but there is no such man. Could you please come with me?" Rising, he took the young nurse and myself, for I was intrigued by this announcement, to the end of the corridor. He illustrated that the door at the end of the corridor was in fact a large store cupboard and not a room at all.

"I definitely saw a man go through that door," said the startled young lady. She was even more startled when the dentist asked her if he was wearing black. Nodding, she sat down with a bump when he told her that this was an apparition and not everyone could see him, though several believed he was the original owner of the house, believed to have died there prior to its sale.

I worked happily at this dental practice for quite some time after this incident and I never did see the man in black, or the young nurse for that matter, as she handed in her notice on the spot and never entered the premises again.

Leah and I had begun to get to know our immediate neighbours, plus we also made a few friends in our respective jobs. At this point, Leah had found a lovely position in a school office and very much enjoyed meeting the staff. One evening she told me she was going for a meal with one of the teaching staff, a very nice chap by the name of Lawrence. The evening was a huge success and soon Leah began to see Lawrence on a regular basis.

One evening there was to be a special dinner dance arranged by the school staff. I was told it was to honour the Headmaster reaching retirement age. Leah would have to buy an evening dress for this event, taking place in a rather swish hotel. Lawrence went with Leah to find this special dress and they came home looking very pleased after their shopping expedition. The dress was indeed lovely, a dark green silk creation with a matching wrap. It suited Leah's colouring beautifully. I was even more impressed when she told me that Lawrence had paid for the dress as a gift. *Wow*, I thought, wishing I had a boyfriend like Lawrence.

Arriving home late from this lovely dinner dance, Leah, seeing that I was not asleep, began to tell me all about the evening and what a treat it had all been. Lawrence had been very attentive and the staff appeared delighted for them to be a twosome. The meal had been wonderful and all in all a terrific night out.

The next morning was Saturday and not a work or school day, so Leah and I had a rather lazy morning spent catching up with more news about the previous evening. I asked if this relationship was serious and would she be considering staying in this country permanently. Leah shook her head and said, "Not a chance, and I have something to tell you. I will at some point be moving on and I'll need to think of a way to end this relationship for the benefit of others."

I was at a loss as to what she could possibly mean, but it eventually transpired that Lawrence was in fact gay, and in the early sixties the situation was decidedly precarious for someone in the teaching profession. Had anyone in the education field discovered this fact he would most definitely have lost his job. He had become close to Leah whilst giving her a lift home from school each day, trusting her with his dilemma. Then he asked her if she would pretend to be his girlfriend. Leah agreed and so the courtship had progressed happily and all was well.

I was shocked to hear that this extremely nice young man had to resort to such lengths to retain his job. He would be very sad to lose Leah, who made life so much easier for him. Sad to think that all these years later, there would still exist situations where honesty might not be the very best policy! It had to be said that this was definitely the time for change. The civil rights movement was in full swing and the second wave feminists were making very big waves. Times really were changing! Today, however, fifty years after all this optimism, riots are still taking place in the U.S. based on black and white conflict, and gay orientation can still make life difficult for many, and women are still fighting in many areas for equality.

LOS ANGELES REVISITED

Sadly, the day came when I said goodbye to Leah and San Francisco. It had been an interesting stay in that fabulous city, to say the least, but I felt I was going home as I packed my suitcase.

Once again I landed in the Los Angeles airport. Little did I know then that that this would be the pattern of my life. I would always find myself drawn back to Los Angeles and have landed in this exciting spot countless times during my lifetime. Audrey and Arthur, who had kept in touch, were going on a fairly long trip and wondered if I would consider returning to look after the boys for them. Yes indeed, I would, and found on arrival the lovely feeling of 'coming home'.

A lady from the supply agency had been hired to be housekeeper and I was to take care of the boys in their absence. It was so good to see them. They had grown, of course, but they were happy to see me too and I knew we would have fun, though it turned out to be more fun than I could have envisioned. The housekeeper, called Frances, had a wicked sense of humour and we got on well together. Frances was a great practical joker and played some lovely little tricks on the boys to make them laugh. They soon loved her too.

One night when the boys were asleep, Frances and I had a coffee and she began to tell me tales of her youth. She had grown up in Chicago in a fairly poor, though happy, family.

One of her ambitions growing up was to travel down the Mississippi on a paddle steamer. It looked so very romantic and she had heard tales of very wealthy people taking these trips. She used to tell her family that one day she would sail on one of these steamboats and find a millionaire. They laughed, of course, but so determined was Frances that one day after she'd turned twenty-one, she booked herself onto a Mississippi steam boat. Everyone was astonished, but admired her spirit and wished her well.

It was a wonderful trip, she told me, and she met some amazing people. At one point of the voyage, as a joke, she sent a telegram to her family saying she had met and married her millionaire and would like to bring him home to meet them. Knowing what a jokester she was, she knew they would roar with laughter. Of course, telegrams happened to be the only means of communication in those days. Families did not even have a land line, so it was fun to send such a message. Three weeks later, Frances arrived home, happy though a little tired after her long trip. She could not wait to see the family and relate all the wonderful stories to them. However, she was confused to arrive home and find the place in darkness, no trace of anyone inside. Her heart sank, thinking they had forgotten the date she was due back.

Opening the door with her key, she pushed through with her case and wandered down the hall into the lounge, and got the shock of her life. The entire family had gathered to give her a surprise welcome-home party. A huge banner was strung across the wall saying "Congratulations to the Newlyweds" and a table groaned under the weight of wedding gifts and food. Bottles of champagne stood waiting to be uncorked and everyone had enormous grins on their faces. For the first time in her life, poor Frances was struck almost dumb, struggling to say, "But I was only joking!"

Telling me this story from so long ago still made her roar with laughter. "You would think that would have taught me a lesson," she said, "but sadly it did not!"

It was a beautiful day and the boys had been to nursery school and were still a little restless. I told Frances they were probably missing their parents and perhaps we should do something to take their minds off the fact. We thought a trip to the beach might be just the thing, and so off we set after lunch, hoping an hour or so on the sand would help run off a little energy.

We drove to the coast, arriving in Santa Monica, but the beach was a little crowded and so it was decided we should drive a little farther up the coast to Malibu. However, driving to Malibu, we were bemused to find crowds on the shoreline, clearly very excited about something happening in the water. Chatting to some onlookers we learned that President Kennedy had gone for a swim with his brother-in-law Peter Lawford. He had been staying with Peter at his beachfront home and they decided to take a dip.

It certainly did not take long for a crowd to form and the excitement was intense. Young ladies squealing with delight followed them into the waves and it appeared they were almost swamped with attention. We strained our eyes for a look at President Kennedy and his brother-in-law but we could not make them out through the crowd. At this point it was quite chaotic, photographers jostling for the best position to take a shot. The crowd moved like ants towards the beachfront houses as the famous twosome, with no little effort, vanished inside.

"How sad," I said to Frances. "I would love to see President Kennedy."

"Maybe another time," she replied. "He must be here on holiday."

The following day we headed for the shops and Farmers' Market. We knew the boys loved that place and we could buy them lunch for a treat. Driving along, we became suddenly aware of a commotion behind us and Frances pulled over to the side of the road and stopped the car. Perhaps an accident, we thought, but suddenly several very important cars drove past, one flying a flag, and we realised that this was indeed the presidential motorcade.

The car sped past and we were treated to the back of the head of the most famous man in the world. "Drat," I told Frances. "That's twice I almost saw the president."

She laughed her reply, saying, "Third time lucky, you never know."

Neither of us could have known there would never be a third chance to see this famous man. In a few short weeks, no one would ever see him again, because the fatal day in Dallas was looming. I recall seeing all the jolly laughing photographs in the press later that day of President Kennedy on the beach taking all the fuss in good spirits. If only we had known what lay ahead, and how the future of the world would have been totally different but for that fateful day in Dallas.

One of the joys of returning to Los Angeles was being reunited with Ethel, the wonderful cook and great companion of Saturday night dinners! There was to be a special party for Audrey's sister, a rapidly rising star and acclaimed artist, celebrating the finishing of her amazing tile mosaic for the children's ward of the Marion Richards centre. It was a most wonderful work of art, filling the whole of the entrance hall with dancing figures of all the well-known children's nursery rhymes. It was truly spectacular and much lauded in the press. A dinner would be organised in her honour and, as usual, it was to take place in the lovely outdoors.

Tables would be under the trees with twinkling lights all over the garden. Ethel would prepare a marvellous dinner, with me taking the role of sorcerer's apprentice. The evening was a great success, with Ethel, as ever, the happy, funny companion. At the end of all the celebrations, to my delight, Ethel invited me to visit her at her house in South Los Angeles. I was thrilled and accepted at once, but it is true to say I had no idea how I would get there.

It would be Ethel's birthday and so all her family would be in attendance, and there were indeed very many in her family. It would be a grand gathering. Ethel had in fact been married three times and given birth to nine children. They in turn presented her with numerous grandchildren. Ethel's first two husbands had died and her current husband was severely disabled, the victim of an industrial accident which left him bedridden. Ethel never complained, saying she was fortunate in her catering skills, which enabled her to find work. She worked day and night to keep the family afloat, but looking after all the children, cleaning, cooking and ferrying them to school was never mentioned, nor the fact that most weekends she would spend the evenings cooking for dinner parties to make ends meet. What a brave lady.

I knew the area I would be visiting was exclusively black and suffered from many problems, but I found it even more interesting for that. Having only experienced the more desirable neighbourhoods up to this point, I thought it splendid that I should get to see the background to other lives in that big city. This visit would redress the balance.

Taking a bus downtown was the easy bit, and Ethel assured me that one of her family would meet me and drive me the rest of the way. True to her word on the appointed day, I stepped down from the bus to find a smiling lady waiting for me. I knew instantly this was Ethel's daughter because she was the positive image of her mother. After a fairly short drive to Ethel's house, I was warmly greeted by the birthday lady and introduced to all her family. Lunch had been set outdoors and what a wonderful feast it was, dishes I had never seen or heard of before, but all delicious.

There was an interesting arrangement outdoors, behind the house. I would have called this the back garden, but in the U.S. it was always referred to as the yard. Several families had combined their back yards, making one large area where all the neighbours could gather and socialise. It was a perfect arrangement for this celebration.

A short while into the celebration, it dawned on me that the guests were all female, not a man in sight, which did seem a little odd. A sudden roar of laughter filled the air and I realised that all the men were outside the yard area, seated in what I would have called an alley! Ethel took me to have a look and, to my astonishment, I found the 'alley' filled with card tables and chairs, some of the men absorbed in card games in progress. It was also pointed out to me that several teenage boys stood 'on guard' at each end of this alley, looking out for any police in the area.

I never did discover what was the exact card game they played, though I was told it was illegal and they would be in a great deal of trouble should the police find out. Ethel's disabled husband had been carried outdoors in a large arm chair from his bed in the corner of the lounge—because he could not manage stairs. He sat amongst the crowd of men, having a whale of a time for a change. Ethel had a marvellous party, music and laughter filling the air. I felt so special to be part of it all. To this day, I think she is the most inspirational person I have ever met.

I discovered Joy, the Scottish girl, was living nearby in Brentwood, still working in her capacity as nanny. We were happy to link up again and decided we would get together on our next day off. She had been given another car by her employer, superior to the initial one, which could only be described as a banger. In those days her job included taking the children to school, so her employers wanted to buy her a reliable vehicle. It was a smooth ride and a real delight, and we realised that we'd be able to go further afield on our days off.

Looking at the map, we decided to drive further down the coast, finding ourselves in Newport Beach one bright sunny day. This was a most attractive little seaside town with lots of lovely boats sailing in and out of the harbour. We had lunch and then sat on a jetty to eat ice cream cones in the sun.

It was at this point that a sweet little boat sailed in and pulled up to the jetty immediately in front of us. A stunningly-handsome young man grinned up at us and threw us the rope saying, "Come, girls, tie this up for me."

We did as we were told, of course. After he jumped onto the jetty, he realised we were Brits and this appeared to tickle him no end. He shouted for his friend Peter, who was still below deck, and said, "We have two new crew members and they are posh Brits!" After tying up the boat, they asked us to join them for a drink in the boat club.

We did not need to be asked twice. Those two were handsome and fun, and quite a find. We discovered that they lived in Pasadena and they would hitch the boat to the back of their car to drive back up the coast. We exchanged phone numbers, intending to meet again. My, we were excited, but my heart sank a little knowing that we both had our eyes on the same chap. Joy had what I could only describe as 'pneumatic appeal' and I did not fancy my chances with Mr Gorgeous.

A week or so went by before Joy received a phone call from the boat owner inviting us to dinner. This was in fact Mr Gorgeous, who went by the name of David. We learned he shared a house with Peter somewhere on top of a hill in

Pasadena. It was an unknown area for us and so we were excited, eagerly looking forward to the dinner. David, it transpired, claimed to be an excellent cook and he gave us directions to the house, promising us an interesting dinner and evening.

The directions appeared fairly straightforward. It would be about twelve miles from our location to Pasadena, but the problem arose of how to find the right house. At this point the map looked a little vague, but we had his phone number should we get lost. At the next opportunity, we set out to visit the two young men. As predicted the main part of the journey was quite straightforward, but then we had to head out of town to find the indicated road. It was very steep, long and twisty, and more than once we doubted the direction. To our relief, we eventually made it to the top of the canyon road and found the house we were looking for.

This turned out to be a doddle because there was only one house at the top of the hill. We were warmly welcomed by the young men, who complimented us on finding them as they ushered us inside. Well, to say it was rough and ready would be an understatement. The house was virtually falling apart. We learned that these two were students and renting this house on a shoestring budget, but they loved the independence it afforded. Peter, in particular, was very keen on wildlife and it abounded right outside their back door. They had a near derelict balcony of rotting wood with a precipitous drop to the canyon floor below. I could not get back into the house quick enough, but the boys laughed and said it was perfectly safe.

The meal was indeed delicious, David telling the truth when he said he could cook. After dinner, much to my unease, we had drinks on the wobbly balcony, and then the inevitable happened. David took Joy's hand and led her away into the little lounge so they could be alone, leaving me on the balcony with Peter. What on earth was I to do? He was nice enough, but not my cup of tea, and I felt great envy of Joy taking off with Mr Gorgeous.

Peter drew close and all I could think was to keep talking! I managed this for a couple of hours until the poor chap finally got the message and said he would go and feed the wildlife underneath the balcony. He disappeared into their little garage to lift out the food and I thankfully escaped. I could find no sign of David or Joy and walked to the front of the house, peering into the now dark night. They eventually appeared, having been for a walk, and looked very cosy indeed.

I told them Peter was feeding the racoons and David nodded, saying, "Yes, every night without fail." Joy and I agreed it was time to leave and I thankfully climbed into her car for the return journey home. The following day, Joy rang to say that David had gone straight to bed, leaving Peter feeding the racoons, or so he thought. Apparently, the balcony had finally collapsed when Peter tried to climb back over it and he had fallen down the canyon, taking the balcony with him where he had been lying injured all night! He had broken many bones and was in hospital in a bad way. I felt so guilty for treating him badly, but thought it Joy's fault for being so pneumatic and attractive!

I should have been wary, considering the escapades with the two boys and the balcony, but Joy was always looking for new adventures. As we would probably only pass by that once, I usually went along with her schemes. The fact that Joy had a rather nice car to drive around made these escapades so much easier to arrange. At that point, we had been rather taken with the concept of a drive-in cinema. It was so new and exciting and now that Joy had a car and a licence to drive it, we determined that our next trip would be to one of those delightful places.

I was learning to drive but did not have a car. It would take me some time before I could take a driving test. It was quite amazing in those days, all you had to do was present yourself at the local police station and as soon as an officer was free he would take you out for a spin. He instructed you about where to go, not very far at all, before then asking you to demonstrate how to park in the police station yard. Afterwards, if he was happy, bingo, you had a licence!

Joy had undergone this procedure several times, but even this relatively easy task appeared to be beyond her. However, one day she announced that she had the desired licence. I congratulated her, saying how well she had done to finally pass the test. She grinned and said that the chap she worked for had friends in high places. Apparently, he rang the station and they issued her with a licence! Hard to believe, but true. This was the early sixties after all.

The cinema trip was now a reality, so with glee, off we drove, with no concern for the fact that Joy really could not drive to save her life, or mine, for that matter!

"We shall have a fun night," Joy said, incorporating the local jargon into her speech with a grin. Negotiating the cinema parking lot did appear to be easy for her, I had to say. We were early and the place had a great deal of parking space. How excited we were to have the sound equipment attached to the window of our car, and then the luxury of ordering food to eat whilst watching the film. It was all rather surreal. We were, it had to be said, just as interested in the other cinema goers as we were in the film, particularly a couple of rather handsome men driving a breathtakingly-impressive Thunderbird sports car.

Towards the end of the film, they began to lean out of their car windows to chat and flirt. Giggling, we went along with it all. Driving out of the car park at the end of the film, we were a little surprised to see the Thunderbird following us and honking the horn. Pulling up at the traffic lights, the men shouted that we should follow them to their place. But we clearly saw them for the first time in the light of the street and realised, with shock, that they were in fact rather older than we'd thought, and a little seedy-looking to boot!

Joy said not to worry, that we would pretend to follow and then disappear down a street somewhere. So, with a cheery wave, we set off and tucked in behind this odd twosome. After only a few moments, Joy turned the car into a side street and we thankfully drove away only to realise almost immediately that the gruesome twosome had executed a U turn and were now following us! Oh my, what on earth should we do?

Joy drove faster, but with no effect, their car much faster than ours, and his driving skills more advanced. On and on went the chase, until we realised that we were totally lost in this vast city and panic setting in. What started out as a fun night, to quote Joy, was fast turning into a scary reality. Completely out of control at this point, Joy was driving along the pavement and, in one swift encounter, managed to flatten several pavement seats of a trendy-looking cafe. A small ornamental fountain was next and I found myself shouting, "Brake, brake!" but to no avail. She was frozen to the accelerator pedal.

Seeing a stone arch appear in our direct line, I thought it best to simply pray hard as the car tried to shoot through this; however, this obviously being a 'pedestrian only' arch, the car was wider than the arch and mercifully Joy had finally taken her foot off the gas. We came to a juddering halt, wedged inside the archway. Mercifully, it had been imitation stone and was, in fact, the entrance to a shopping precinct. Thank heaven it was now late at night and no one in the direct line of fire. A car stopped directly behind us, not the Thunderbird, I saw with only partial relief, because it was a police car.

A very stern police officer walked towards us. "Do you want to tell me what happened?" he said.

I wondered just how long he had to listen. To sum up, we were stuck fast in a car wedged at the entrance of a pedestrian shopping mall, an imitation stone arch falling around the mercifully stationary car, totally lost and trying to explain what we were doing there. It was a night to remember, and certainly the last time I ever entered a drive-in cinema!

At that point in time, I think it is fair to say that we were all innocents abroad. It took a good while, and lots of experience, before we heard our wake-up call. For Joy this came one sunny afternoon while home alone. She was preparing the afternoon tea before collecting the children from school. Answering the door bell, she found a rather smart, sophisticated older man standing there asking if her employer was at home. He had an appointment with him. Joy had to say that no, she was home alone, but he was welcome to come inside and wait. A cup of coffee was proffered and accepted whilst he told Joy that he was a business acquaintance of the man of the house and they were about to form an alliance.

Joy was impressed, and indeed he did look the part in his very smart suit. He chatted for some considerable time before taking his leave and saying he would be in touch with the man of the house later by telephone. "You have been a charming companion and I would love to take you out for dinner," he said.

Blushing, Joy accepted. It was arranged that he would pick her up the following evening and they would find a lovely popular place to have dinner. Telling her employers about the man, Joy was a little confused when they insisted they couldn't bring anyone of that description to mind, though Joy thought it was her fault because she had completely forgotten his name.

The following evening, Joy waited by the front door, eagerly awaiting her smart older man. The very moment a car pulled into the drive, she shot out, excited to be off and begin the sophisticated evening. It was a huge success, the man charming and attentive and Joy thought the considerable age gap did not matter, especially as he was clearly a wealthy individual. Maybe this was her destiny. A couple of dates followed, and on the third occasion the man suggested she pack her bags and leave with him for a life elsewhere in California, naming a particularly expensive location.

"I have a house there," he told Joy. "We can begin a new life in the manner which you deserve."

I do think Joy had reservations, but she decided to pack her belongings and sneak away, entranced by the prospect of finding her millionaire. Joy never mentioned her assignations with this chap to anyone. On the day of departure, she told one of our group by telephone about their plans. Alarm bells rang and this perceptive friend phoned Joy's employer. Acting on the information at once and finding Joy packing, her employer demanded to know the whole story and listened carefully to a tearful Joy.

She finally asked when this man had first arrived at the house, and when Joy told her, giving a more detailed description of the man, plus his name, the lady gasped with astonishment, asking if this was the man claiming to be a business associate.

"Why, yes," Joy replied. "I told you he was a business acquaintance."

The lady of the house reached into her handbag and produced a business card with writing and small photograph on it. "Here is your millionaire," she said.

Joy took the card and with shock saw that her millionaire was in fact a painter and decorator who had called on the chance of employment. Furious and embarrassed, she rang the number only to have the phone slammed down on her. A valuable lesson for a vulnerable young girl. She certainly grew up with considerable speed after that incident.

The summer was extremely hot, the children delighted it was the holiday period and they did not have to attend school. Joy looked after two children, a boy and a girl who were considerably older than my charges. The boy was twelve and the girl thirteen, and so they had very distinctive ideas as to how their day should be spent. The parents told Joy one morning that they wanted to go to Disneyland for the day. Joy rang me and asked if I would like to accompany them, knowing it was my day off from work. I decided it would be a good idea. After all, this place was legendary and, at least at that time, the only one in the world.

Certainly, this was the original theme park and everyone assured me it was not a place to be missed. The first glimpse took your breath away, enormous and the treats on display endless. So much to see and do, Joy's charges were thrilled beyond words, however, I quickly learned this gigantic park had a gigantic problem. So many people attended daily that the queues were mind-blowingly long! Notices everywhere warned us that the wait would be an hour or more, so with sinking hearts we had no choice but to join the end of these never-ending snakes of people.

The heat became intense and I thought I would pass out at any moment. Eventually we would reach the end of this queue and the children would climb aboard. We were too faint-hearted and chose to sit and watch these spine-chilling rides, and the whole time it's getting hotter and hotter!

At last the evening was approaching and the day cooled off a little. I asked if we could leave, but was informed that the best part of the day was about to begin, namely the parade. Darkness fell and brought some relief as we waited, mercifully seated, for the parade to begin. My goodness it was a spectacular sight, floats of every kind imaginable, Disney characters in sparkly costumes, and thousands of fairy lights and fireworks.

I turned to Joy. "You are right, this was the best part of the day. Will we be going home now?"

"Oh, no," she replied. "Now is the best treat of all. Believe me, you will love the next surprise."

My heart sank. I had experienced more than enough of Disneyland, knowing that even though it had been an amazing experience it would not be one I should be repeating. Joy pulled us towards a concert area and found us seats with the tickets she had obviously pre-booked. Sighing, I sat down, relieved only by the fact that I should not have to stand again.

There was a fanfare as the crowd cheered and to my amazement, Louis Armstrong came on to the stage!

Awesome, what a concert it proved to be, a once in a lifetime experience. I sat open-mouthed with wonder as Joy laughed at me. I had at one point told her how highly I thought of this man and his talent, and she had arranged the tickets for me. What an amazing night, never to be forgotten, and worth all that standing in the hot sun to be rewarded by such a thrilling evening.

A BRUSH WITH ART

I confess that in my early days I was a definite philistine when it came to art appreciation. Not having had much talent at school for the subject, I left it to others to practise. I think this was rather disappointing for my father, a talented artist who had a nice side-line in political cartoons he sold to newspapers. His brother also excelled at art, a commercial artist. Several of my family members were very talented, and even today both my daughters display considerable artistic talent.

I am living proof that this talent skips generations! Audrey, however, was very keen and displayed considerable knowledge on the subject. Her role on the Arts Council of Los Angeles was a position she took seriously, not to mention enjoyed immensely. One afternoon Audrey arrived home after such a meeting, happy and excited to announce that the famous Picasso, no less, would hold an exhibition in Los Angeles. The great man had submitted a drawing for the front of the catalogue. To my untutored eye this looked decidedly over-simplified, being as I recall a daisy scrawled in the centre of the cover. It would be a huge event and there certainly would be a huge demand for tickets—the year of the great Picasso exhibition.

It was a first copy of the much-admired cover and I stared at it with confusion as Audrey rang several friends to relate the good news. At this point, Danny came in from the garden, where he had been tiger-spotting from the top of the climbing frame. "Seen any tigers yet?" I asked.

He shook his head with disappointment. "Maybe they will be around later."

I offered him a drink and went to make a little snack as he climbed onto a dining table chair.

Taking his crayons, he coloured in the daisy and added grass, a sun and a bird or two—and what a wonderful transformation, a great improvement in my opinion. Audrey, however, gazed in open-mouthed horror. She would now somehow have to secure another copy to process for the exhibition! I think she secretly preferred Danny's version too, but merely shook her head as he put his crayons aside and returned to tiger hunting in the garden.

Shortly after this incident, I received a phone call from Frances (who had been working a few weeks as chef for a man and wife in Bel Air). Apparently, she had helped at this household in the past, telling me they were simply lovely people. She had related to them her tales of au pairs arriving from England to work in Los Angeles. Intrigued, they instructed Frances to invite Val and me to go for a swim in their luxurious pool—a good opportunity for us to meet up again with Val, of course.

We were thrilled and took up their offer as soon as we were able. A beautiful house met our eyes and the garden had the biggest swimming pool we had ever seen in Los Angeles, and that was saying a lot! Chatting happily, the lovely couple asked lots of questions about England and why we had decided to work in California. Leaving for lunch, they instructed us to make ourselves at home and swim for as long as we wished. We had such fun and I was particularly impressed by the changing rooms in the garden, sheer luxury. They even contained spare swim suits for anyone who wished to borrow one. Towels, plus tea, coffee and boxes of cookies helped the day go along wonderfully well, or should I say swimmingly!

The notice in the changing room made me laugh. It said: "We don't swim in your toilet, please don't pee in our pool."

The afternoon wore on and we eventually left the pool and dressed, just as the householders returned. We thanked them profusely and said how much we enjoyed our afternoon. At this point the gentleman asked if we liked art. "Oh, yes indeed," Val replied, for she most certainly did. I merely nodded out of politeness.

"Follow me," he instructed, and we went into the large house where he and his wife led us up several staircases to the very top of the building. Taking a key from his pocket, he unlocked the door. There in front of us was a huge art gallery, etchings and paintings all along each side of this long gallery. It was fascinating, and I must confess to loving the experience, and indeed loving some of the art work. This kind man spent a great deal of time talking about his collection, which he clearly adored and was very proud of. At last we thanked the gentleman profusely for his kindness and said our goodbyes, an interesting afternoon that we would remember fondly.

Arriving home, I began to relate the activities of the day to Audrey, who listened politely until I reached the part where we were invited to see the art gallery. Not for the first time, Audrey's mouth dropped open. "I do not believe it!" she said. (And you thought Victor Meldrew invented that one! Not so, Audrey used it almost weekly whilst I stayed with them!) On hearing the name of this generous chap, she told me in amazement that the art collection was the largest and most prestigious in private hands in the United States, and also the most coveted. People in the art world would give an arm and a leg to be able to see it—few were ever allowed to view this superb collection. We had been casually invited, to the astonishment of Audrey. Talk about innocents abroad!

The three boys continued to be a delight, Jonathan rather serious and sensitive, Danny full of mischief and very funny whilst keeping a straight face. Baby Robbie chuckled at the other two and was the happiest of babies. One day Audrey told me that Jonathan would be going to the hospital the following week for a minor operation on his ears. He was very brave and all went well, until the moment of his release. The ears had been bandaged with a broad bandage crossing at the front and looking exactly like a like a turban. Jonathan hated it, vowing he would not go outdoors where he could be seen by all and sundry. Fortunately, Audrey had a very talented sister, Elaine, a professional artist and full of interesting ideas.

This problem proved a challenge for her, but she rose to the occasion and told Audrey to stop by her house on leaving the hospital. Sometime later, the car arrived with Jonathan smiling and waving as he stepped out and ran up the front steps. He looked wonderful. Aunt Elaine had worked her magic and placed a large coloured jewel in the middle of the bandage. She attached feathers behind it, cascading from the central point, and he looked like a Sultan. Everyone clapped and complimented him, saying how wonderful he looked and we had one very happy little boy.

It could have been this magnificent headgear that inspired Danny, I cannot be sure, but a short time later he arrived home from nursery school wearing an old, rather battered, bowler hat! To say he looked comical was an understatement, but how he loved it, so much so that he refused to remove it at any point, bath time becoming a challenge. Seeing him in bed wearing pyjamas and a bowler hat was a real treat.

Several days went by and the bowler stayed firmly on Danny's head. His amused parents declared that the end was nigh because they were attending a wedding that coming weekend and he would have to take the hat off when he wore his lovely smart new outfit. You would think that would be the case, but no, the hat stayed firmly in place and off they went to the very smart wedding, all looking perfect and Danny still in the bowler hat. Incidentally, I had to also check his pockets were empty. He had a habit of taking his pet terrapin with him in his pocket. I would point out that he should stay in his tank on many occasions, but Danny insisted that, "Walter likes to accompany me on outings!"

WE ARE SAILING

The letters from home began to worry me considerably and I realised that a visit home would have to be arranged. My father had undergone several major operations and did not appear to be improving a great deal, in and out of hospital to his and my mother's distress. It was far less expensive to sail in those days as air travel, still not for the masses, cost an arm and a leg. I secured a place on Cunard Line's *Queen Elizabeth,* set to sail from New York to Southampton. First, of course, I would have to take a cross country flight to New York and, I must confess, the thought of visiting this wonderful city thrilled me. I decided to spend a week there before joining the ship.

Flying east, I found myself sitting next to a young man in U.S. Army uniform and we fell into conversation. He told me he was going home on leave after a foreign tour. When I asked where, he told me Vietnam. I had to scratch my head to recall exactly where that was. Decidedly confused, I asked why on earth the United States would have troops in such a country?

"Oh, it is just a small task force," he replied. "We're only there for a short while." You can probably imagine in the years to come how that conversation resonated.

Landing in New York, I was reminded of the time of my speechless arrival fiasco and pondered all that had transpired since. I found the Y.W.C.A. in Lexington Ave. and was eagerly anticipating my week in this exciting city, planning to explore and enjoy the sights. The hostel was lovely, and actually clean and spacious, the staff very friendly and helpful. I took my luggage to my allocated room and found a rather morose-looking girl sitting on one of the other beds. I smiled hello but received no response. Feeling rather hungry, I took my leave and went to look for something to eat. Such a wonderful array of places to eat met my eyes. I soon learned about 'deli heaven' and thoroughly enjoyed my snack as I wandered around the area.

I thought New York wonderful, in that you did not have any need to drive, or indeed to use any form of transport. Unlike Los Angeles, where if you walked, people assumed you were looking for help, it was all doable on foot. I bought a map and looked for locations of all the special places I longed to see. I made a note of the priorities for the following day, but it was getting late at this point and I did feel tired. Making my way back to the hostel, I pondered on just how very different the big cities of this vast country were. Arriving at the hostel, I found the room empty, and that pleased me thinking a good night's sleep was ahead. I had, however, seen a notice on the stairs saying ROOF and suddenly felt attracted, craving a peep at New York City from a lofty position at night.

Stepping out onto the roof was magical, the air balmy, and all around the lights twinkled. I then became aware of a figure to the side of me, sitting near the edge of the perimeter wall with her leg raised to climb over to the street below. I froze, finding the dour girl who had been sitting on my bed earlier. Nothing could have prepared me for such an occasion and I had no idea what on earth I should do next.

The girl, sensing my presence, turned her head and slowly said, "No point in trying to stop me. I am going to end it all."

I replied, "Why?" which was indeed a genuine reply, because I was wondering exactly why she would be in this situation. To my surprise, she began to talk, and I slowly walked towards her. It turned out that she had met an American guy in her native Canada and fallen instantly in love. This was, she told me, the love of her life and when he said he must return to New York, she became distraught. He told her she was welcome to return to New York with him and, thrilled at the thought, she drew all her savings from her bank account, telling no one when she took off with the young man. Her life, she said, had been sad. Orphaned at a young age, she had lived with a distant aunt who had no time for her. On reaching her late teens, shy and miserable and in a dead-end job with no prospect of change, the young man appeared in her life. The most exciting thing that had ever happened to her.

Having once visited Buffalo with her aunt, she did have a passport so, beyond excited, she climbed into the young man's car, all her possession in a small suitcase, along with her passport and all the money she had in the world. Not a huge amount, but it did represent her entire savings. They laughed and sang to the radio as they sped towards the crossing point into the U.S. from Canada. Everything went swimmingly and they drove on south to New York City. On the outskirts of the city they stopped to eat in a diner and the girl realised she was tired as well as hungry. By then the adrenaline rush had fizzled out and she found herself suddenly very weary. The love of her life laughed, telling her to put her head down for a little while whilst he ordered coffee and a piece of pie to finish their meal. She placed her head on the table and instantly fell asleep.

Waking with a jolt sometime later, as the waitress gently shook her shoulder, she discovered her young man had gone, taking her suitcase, handbag, money and passport with him. Distraught, she had no idea what to do next and burst into tears. Her tears turned to sobs and howls of distress. An elderly couple sitting at a nearby table came over to try and comfort her. On hearing her story, they told her to get into their car and they would try to help. She had no choice but to trust them, and mercifully they were true to their word and drove her into the city and straight to the Y.W.C.A. They then paid for a night's lodging, telling her to go to the police first thing in the morning. The entire situation had overcome her and she could see no point in going on.

At this point, I found myself standing next to her as she contemplated climbing over the ledge into the abyss. Swiftly, I put my arms around her and pulled back from the ledge, hurling her backwards with great force due to panic on my part. We sat in a heap on the floor of the roof and I knew I would have to talk fast if I wanted any hope of changing her mind. I felt if she was determined enough, she might jump up, run away from me and leap over the edge.

After some time and catching our breath, I realised she would be fine and slowly released her from my vice-like grip. The poor girl began to sob and I felt helpless, clueless at this point as to what to do. Urging her to her feet, I led her to the stairs and we descended to the front lobby. There was no one to be seen, the place deserted and very quiet indeed. I found myself silently praying for help and felt sure her guardian angel must have heard, because suddenly the most inspirational thought filled my head and I found myself asking if she had a religion.

"Yes, I am a Catholic," she replied. On questioning her further, I was able to elicit that until a few years ago, she had attended church on a fairly regular basis.

"Right," I said, jumping to my feet and pulling her to hers. "Follow me." Meekly, she did as I bid and we went out onto the street, where earlier on my walk I had noticed a Catholic church not too far away.

Pulling her as gently as I could, and keeping a tight hold of her arm, we found the church and went inside. There, like a guiding light, stood a priest and two ladies who looked up startled as we approached. Several hours later, after re-telling her long story, tea and cake and much sympathy ensued. This little group told me to go and that they would look after her, assuring me they would take good care of her.

I walked back to the hostel and, thank goodness, was allowed to enter when I rang the bell even though it was in the early hours of the morning at this point. I began to shake with the realisation of what had happened that night, certainly saying my prayers before I fell into bed. Calling the next day at the Church, I found all was underway to rescue this young lady. She would be staying with one of the Church ladies, who would take care of her and unravel her considerable problems with care and compassion. Phew, such a relief.

After a shaky start, the week following was quite wonderful. I visited all the sights, gazing out from the observation platforms of the Empire State Building the highlight, almost surreal. As I explored, all those films I had seen set in New York flooded through my head. Central Park was a wonder and I spent hours walking around, mainly people-watching. In the very centre was a carousel and I found myself riding this with the excitement of a three-year-old. There was something quite magical about the glittery old painted horses, plus the distinctive jolly music, all quite lovely.

At the end of one afternoon, I sat on a park bench and ate a sandwich before exiting onto the west side of the park. When I returned to the park many years later, I realised that I had in fact been sitting in the exact spot where, sadly, the future memorial to John Lennon would be placed. Years later, I viewed the simple, yet beautiful, circular mosaic with the single word "Imagine" written in the centre.

It was, however, time to leave and the following morning I made my way to the docks filled with excitement and anticipation.

Walking down the covered awning to the gangway, I emerged into daylight at the bottom and found myself at the side of the ship, totally astonished at the sheer size of it. Gazing up and up, it appeared to tower skywards forever, a positive behemoth of a vessel. I remembered this feeling later, in the middle of the Atlantic, when the waves were so enormous the ship appeared as if a plastic toy ship in one's bath, riding up the cliff of water, tipping over the top, and hurtling down the other side. My goodness, it made one feel small and put many of my worries into perspective.

I found my cabin and discovered I would be sharing it with a very sweet elderly lady, who apparently had been visiting her son in New York City. We shook hands and exchanged pleasantries, but this initial meeting would be the last time I saw her vertical until we reached Southampton. She had said, in passing, that she was a poor sailor and my goodness was that an understatement. The dear lady never left her bunk after the first few hours afloat and survived on dry toast and water for the five and a half days it took us to arrive in the U.K. The steward or myself would offer cups of tea or coffee, but even this proved too much of a challenge and she sipped water and slept all the way across the Atlantic.

Sailing past the Statue of Liberty proved to be a very moving experience and I found myself thinking of all the people who had arrived and departed that great city. Sailing past Ellis Island with all that history, my thoughts turned to visions of many people arriving with just a small bag of belongings, trying to escape a dreadful life to begin again. Today, I never hear the wonderful song by Neil Diamond *Coming to America* without visualising sailing that day from New York.

The first evening, I made my way to the dining hall and found my name placed on a table with a dozen young people all approximately the same age as myself. This was very pleasing and soon we were all chatting gaily, exchanging stories of why and how we came to be leaving America. We had been handed a programme of events for this ship and it seemed there was something of interest virtually every waking hour. A film show kept us amused that evening, but as most people were a little tired at this point, and the weather was turning rough, we all said goodnight and went to our respective bunks.

The following morning, waking was a revelation of how the sea might change in a very short space of time. The slightly rolling sea of the night before had become a tossing and heaving one. Just walking proved to be a challenge. The crew had tied ropes, or lines, along the corridors for us to grab, helping us to make our way along safely. I made my way to the dining room holding on to anything at hand. We were told that this was shaping up to be the worst storm in many a year. In the dining room, our greeting was the sound of breaking pots and plates as they began to hurl themselves onto the floor. The waiter said they would be strapping everything down in the kitchen and we must take care. The tables had flaps on the edges that you could turn up to form a ledge and prevent plates full of food from hitting the deck, literally. He told us, with studied understatement, that this was probably one of the first big storms of the winter.

Looking around the dining room, I noticed the place was virtually empty, only those with rather strong stomachs had made it that morning. Breakfast, however, was delicious, despite being offered sheep's brains for the first time in my life. What a sight that was on a moving table! We were informed, by one who knew these things, that there was a sneaky way to reach the first-class area, where we could find more things to interest us. Classes were severely segregated in those days, so we were advised to make our way up to first class at the earliest possible moment to make our faces known, then we would probably not be apprehended.

After the meal, several of the young people, including myself, decided to go on deck and see the waves. Oh, my goodness, what a sight met our eyes. Huge waves tossed the ship and I thought of all the comments I had heard about stabilisers and no need to worry about wave motion. Ha! Holding on for dear life, but laughing uncontrollably, we decided to walk around the deck. This was certainly bracing and very few other people had ventured outside with us.

Locating the secret way to the upper decks, we struggled up the violently-moving stairway to reach first class. However, there was a lone man slowly making his way along the deck, clearly a first-class passenger. Clutching the rails, he lurched towards us and, once alongside, beamed and wished us a good morning. To our astonishment, we saw it was Bob Hope! We met him every morning after that. No matter how rough the sea, he would take his morning lunge across the decks. Always friendly, on some days he even stopped for a little chat.

Several of the young American people on board were sailing to the U.K. to take up positions in universities where they would study for the middle year of their degree course. All of them appeared to be heading for different cities, and one lovely young lady announced that she was headed for Manchester and asked if I knew the city. I assured her I did indeed, this being my home city, and instantly we forged a friendship. Sally and I were destined to be friends for life.

The days rolled on, literally, because the storm showed no sign of abating. Fewer people than ever made it to the dining room, and soon you could count the people still able to eat on two hands! We had heard during the week that Chubby Checker was on board and demonstrating his huge hit of that summer— The Twist! We heard that one evening a middle-aged lady twisting the night away with excessive vigour died on the spot of a heart attack. Apparently, the following day she was buried at sea.

To our surprise and delight, on the last day before arriving in Southampton, all folk still standing received an invitation for a drinks reception in the private rooms of Bob Hope! Tickled pink, we all went along without being asked twice. He was charming, chatting to us all, and appeared to be enjoying the occasion as much as we were. So much excitement had been planned for the last night, including an announcement for a dance in the ballroom later in the evening. Buoyed by several drinks, a group of us made our way to the ballroom, where yet another surprise met us. There indeed was the famous Chubby Checker leading all who dared in The Twist. We peeped in, not having suitable attire for twisting, though perhaps we were put off by the demise of the lady earlier in the week. It might also have been the fact that we were aware that our 'cover' might be blown and we would be exposed as lower-deck folk.

The following morning found us sad and excited in equal measure as we collected our suitcases to be ready for customs. My dear little old lady had finally put her wobbly feet to the floor and declared she had never been so happy to see dry land. I certainly believed her, and it was good to see her complexion back to normal after the green hue of the past few days. I had already said goodbye to my companions, ensuring Sally had my telephone number. Due to the pressure of my dad's illness, my mother mercifully had a telephone installed. There was one young man I had grown close to during the week, a rather studious chap with horn-rimmed glasses, and I found that quite attractive. We had chatted a great deal and I was pleased to hear he came from the north of England. Going home after a year studying in New York, he too was sad, though happy to be home again.

As we disembarked, we realised we had not exchanged details and he said we must sit together on the train to London. Delighted, I agreed, but as we descended to the end of the gangway we were all decanted into queues dictated by the initial of our last names. My name was Thaw and so I was directed to the very end of the hall to check through customs. The attractive student must have had a name beginning with A, because he was sent to the very opposite end of the giant hangar-like room. Ushered through this procedure, we were then shunted with haste onto the waiting train. I had no choice but to comply and sat next to a window looking for the young man. Glancing around, I saw at this point the rather distraught-looking young man having to open and display all his luggage, red-faced and angry as the whistle blew and the train pulled away. Who knows what might have transpired, but I never saw him again.

ADVENTURES WITH SALLY

I did see Sally again. Settling into her term at Manchester University was rather difficult, everything strange for her. The 'preppy' scene she had been used to at home was far removed from student life in Manchester. We met in the city and she was thrilled to chat about her new life, and indeed her reservations about it. Students wore high heels and tights, was her first observation, and they appeared to take life a good deal more seriously. This proved not to be the case, but her first impression was of a more grown-up serious group of young people.

Sally made friends quickly and soon began to find her way around the city. One day she told me that two of her friends had gone to study in Edinburgh and loved the city. They had written inviting her to visit, so she asked if I'd like to go with her. Well, I had to admit I had never been so far north and it was a most attractive prospect.

"We shall be able to stay in their student house," Sally added. "There is an attic bedroom we are welcome to stay in." The visit was arranged and as the weather was turning cold we planned our outfits accordingly. Wrapped warmly in scarf and gloves, we set off by train for the great adventure north. Sally's friends were delighted to see us and catch up with all the news.

Anxious to show us the delights of Edinburgh, we were marched at once round this hilly, and decidedly chilly, city.

The wind-chill factor made it feel like an Arctic expedition. We became so cold that Sally declared her very head was frozen. At last, after a warming meal, we headed home for the student house. It was tall, granite grey and rather foreboding, and not terribly warm, though lots of laughter and hot chocolate followed and we were soon warmed by the company alone.

Eventually it was time for bed and we were led up the narrow stairs to the attic room. Ye, Gods, it was freezing! I had never been in a room so cold before, or since, come to think of it. It took a brave effort to undress and pull on pyjamas, but we made swift work of it and dived into bed. Wishing each other good night, we tried to sleep, though clearly it would be impossible. Suddenly Sally said she was going to put her sweater back on. This sounded like a very sensible plan so I did the same. Sometime later we added a scarf, woolly socks and gloves, but eventually the only solution was to get into bed together, arctic travellers clinging to each other for dear life!

Returning to Manchester, we found news that the entire country was held in the grip of an arctic blast, and though Manchester was as cold as Edinburgh we did at least have warm buildings. Actually, it was the start of the dreaded 1963 winter, legendary now in weather records as one of the worst winters ever.

Excited about the soon arrival of the festive season, Sally concentrated hard on her studies. She became quite thrilled about the prospect of her parents coming to England for the Christmas holidays. My father, home from hospital and feeling well, was delighted to meet Sally and it was arranged that her family would visit us for Christmas day. How lovely, warm and wonderful her parents proved to be.

Sally's mother arrived holding with great care a long, flat box. She announced, "I have carried these by hand all the way from the U.S." The box contained a big surprise, a special homemade gift from Sally's sister-in-law, who was particularly talented in homemade crafts. She told us that we should never guess what was inside the box.

At this point, Sally's mother handed her the box to give to my mother, saying, "Happy Christmas."

Sally would be teased for the rest of her life over what happened next. She dropped the box, clearly breaking the contents. She said loudly, "Drat, I broke the candles!" So much for 3,000 miles of careful handling and secrecy. The festivities, however, were terrific fun and the family said goodbye, issuing an invitation for us all to visit them in Ohio, and indeed, one day we would!

The winter passed with speed and soon Easter arrived to brighten our days. I received a phone call from my Los Angeles family saying that they would be visiting London with the boys and could I possibly meet them. *Try and stop me,* I thought, looking forward to seeing them all. I missed them so much. They would, it transpired, be staying at the *Connaught Hotel* and suggested I meet them there for lunch. I set off with great excitement, traveling down to London from Manchester in perfect time for lunch.

On entering the foyer of their hotel, the first thing I saw was Jonathan and Daniel, both wearing football outfits, hurtling towards me. It seemed like only yesterday I had seen them, but my goodness how they had grown. Audrey, Arthur and Robbie followed behind, and after a good hug we went into the dining room for lunch. The Connaught was a rarefied, if a little stuffy, atmosphere, which the boys thankfully lifted as soon as they entered. We found our table and ordered from the delicious menu whilst chatting and catching up on all the news.

I looked up and noticed a wonderfully-dressed, elegant lady walking towards us. She stopped to say hello to Audrey and Arthur on her way to her dining table. They had a brief chat whilst I wondered who this lady reminded me of. She seemed so very familiar, especially her voice. As she moved away, I remarked to Audrey that I could not possibly know such a fantastic-looking lady, but she was nevertheless familiar.

Audrey laughed, saying she was not at all surprised. I thought her familiar because it was in fact Princess Lee Radziwill, sister of Jackie Kennedy! Audrey and Arthur had teased me a lot in Los Angeles about initially being so star struck. I am pleased to say that this passed after some period and I realised that these stars were people just like everyone else, with just as many, if not more, everyday problems as the rest of us. However, having said that, there was one famous star I longed to meet, and who never failed to turn me to jelly every time I saw him on the screen. This was Paul Newman.

Arthur would see him all the time and often come home in the evening with a big grin, saying, "Saw the short guy again today, Glennyce." Compared to Arthur, who was at six-foot-three distinctly tall, Paul Newman appeared short, but he said it to tease me, I know.

After our Connaught lunch, it was suggested we go to their rooms to freshen up, and for Audrey to change her shoes in preparation for the afternoon's sightseeing around London. There did appear to be an air of mischief around these two and I was a little suspicious when they told me to go and knock on the door of the suite of rooms down the corridor.

"Whatever for?" I asked, but they insisted I go, instructing me to pretend I was looking for them. Just ask *is this the Greenberg suite?* they said. You will see why soon enough. I was, of course, intrigued at this point, and though somewhat puzzled went to knock on the door of the suite next to theirs. After only a slight pause, I heard footsteps approaching the door. It opened and there stood Paul

Newman! In a state of embarrassed confusion, I blurted out that I was looking for the Greenberg family. Replying with a smile that melted my heart, he pointed down the corridor and said, "Next door along, Ma'am."

When I think of today's technological gadgets and 'selfies' I could weep, but the memory is with me forever. I think on reflection, however, I missed the biggest star of them all. Whenever I visited Audrey and Arthur over the years, at some point while out and about in the car, we would sooner or later bump into a celebrity. We would all laugh about my early days and how star-struck I had been.

On one occasion, I arrived at their home with my overnight bag to be greeted by Audrey with a big smile on her face. "Oh my, you should have been here last night," she said. It transpired that they had been giving a dinner party and invited their good friend George Hamilton. "Do bring a friend," they had urged. Imagine the look on their faces when George arrived with Elizabeth Taylor! Now that really would have fazed me!

Going back to my encounter with Paul, we had such a good laugh when I returned to Audrey's and Arthur's rooms, and I said that despite being mortified it was the best experience of my life to date!

Not many celebrities fazed me, but many years later, I found myself filming a series for Sky Television with the lovely Gloria Hunniford. Gloria was, of course, a television legend in the U.K. and I was full of admiration for her. This series had been devised and inspired by the lovely, and hugely successful, Dianne Nelmes of Liberty Bell Television. We met several times when I was a guest on *This Morning*.

Dianne introduced me to Gloria Hunniford, who was to present the television series. We chatted a great deal whilst waiting to go on set for this live television series and I asked her, "Of all the people you have met in show business, who most impressed you?" I knew, after her long career in show business, that she must have been put in contact with just about everyone. She told me that perhaps the most amazing interview she ever conducted was with Doris Day, who had, after years of stardom, become something of a recluse. She had not given an interview in many years and Gloria was amazed to be granted access to this legendary star. Her account of travelling all the way to California for the interview was a wonderful story and I was very impressed indeed. Gloria, of course, had taken it all in her stride.

I was constantly amazed at the spin-off events surrounding the publication of a book. It led me to people and events that surprised and delighted me. At the end of my television series with Gloria, I had the lovely experience of being included in lots of radio broadcasts while accompanying her. We even flew to Edinburgh to meet the people at Sky and spend the day meeting and greeting. One radio broadcast proved to be quite magical, so very different from any I had done before.

I was invited to be guest on the late-night James Whale programme. Everyone warned me that James was a barracuda and I should be very afraid. I went on air for the live phone-in programme at around eleven P.M. and instantly took a liking to James. He was nothing but kind and helpful to me, especially when the phone calls began to arrive thick and fast. We eventually came off air at one-thirty A.M. and I was to be driven home to my hotel along with my publicity assistant.

We crossed the River Thames, the bridge twinkly and empty, and you could look downriver to all the bridges and buildings, twinkling and floodlit. London appeared to be totally empty, almost surreal, though breathtakingly beautiful. It is my most treasured memory of London, and indeed the James Whale show.

One unexpected and fun event I became involved in was the Publishers' Dinner. Publishers, book sellers and authors were assembled in various locations around the U.K. After a wonderful dinner at an impressive hotel, authors were introduced to the assembled guests. Afterwards, we had to circulate amongst the book sellers. The idea being that if the book sellers found an author particularly engaging they would order more of their book. It was known as "pressing the flesh".

Well, I went along to my very first such prestigious dinner in Manchester, held at the lovely Lowry Hotel. It promised to be a wonderful night with lots of guests and authors present. I arrived, wandering in the hotel lobby a little confused as to where I should go next. Suddenly, I spied a notice at the foot of the stairs saying *Publishers' Dinner* with a large arrow pointing to the right and up the stairs. Assuming the dining hall was on the first floor, I tripped up the stairs only to be confronted by a long corridor clearly comprised of bedrooms. Before I could decide my next move, a bedroom door opened and a man appeared, walking towards the lift. Without a second thought, I launched into a chat about how I was looking for the Publishers' Dinner and did he know where it might be taking place. He gave me a rather bored stare but said the dining room was on the first floor, and with that stepped into the lift. I swiftly followed him and asked if he would be attending too. A nod of yes followed and when I looked closely, I thought to myself, *oh goodness, no wonder he does not want to talk*. It was Keith Richards of the *Rolling Stones*!

Deciding to shut up, I merely followed him until we came to the dining room where everyone was assembled, sitting at elegantly-set tables. As we walked through the door, a huge cheer went up and all the young male book sellers broke out into frenzied clapping. Well, I mused, I had no idea Keith Richards had written a book, but it was obviously popular.

I enjoyed a wonderful dinner and then a representative from the publisher began to introduce the authors one by one. We went up to the front of the room in alphabetical order and were politely clapped. Suddenly it was the turn of my new pal. He stood up when the lady said, "Howard Marks" and the cheers began again!

Oh my, no wonder he had dismissed me with a hard stare, because the chap I thought was a Rolling Stone was in fact the famous Oxford-educated, international drug dealer! He had written a book about his exploits, including, I imagine, his time in a notorious prison in the U.S. after he had been captured. I was only too glad I had not called him 'Keith' and asked for an autograph!

ITCHING TO GO

I sometimes think I was born with itchy feet, certainly my mother believed this to be true, telling me she could scarcely let me out of sight or I would be off in some direction or other. I grew up surrounded by an extended family. In fact, apart from a couple of exceptions, we all lived on the same street and were incredibly close. The exceptions, I might add, only lived minutes away. Napoleon would have described us as a 'family of shopkeepers'! Aunts, Uncles and indeed grandparents could be found in their respective shops serving everything to the public, from fruit and vegetables, fish and flowers, sweets and tobacco, millinery, groceries, outdoor beer commodities and even funeral services. All life's requirements sorted.

I had many interesting cousins and playmates. Childhood sunny days were spent in the local park all summer long. I must say, cider with Rosie this was not! Far from that bucolic idyll, we were in fact definitely 'townies' but the close proximity of the large park gave us a great deal of freedom. A bottle of lemonade with the odd sandwich and we were good to go for the day.

One summer springs to mind, the hot sunny weather making my feet itch even more than usual and I longed to go to the seaside. I had a word with a couple of friends and suggested we try to find our way to the coast. They agreed. After pooling our meagre spends, we hopped on a trolley bus into the centre of the city. The four of us, perhaps no more than seven or eight years old at this point, found ourselves a little stumped as to which direction we would find the coast from the centre of Manchester. We gazed at the buses in the large bus station, reading the list of place names, but none mentioned Blackpool, our desired destination.

Suddenly, one of my little pals saw a bus with Bolton on the front and she excitedly proclaimed that this was the one we required. She assured us that her aunt lived in Bolton and she knew for a fact that it was near the seaside. With great joy, we jumped aboard and peered through the windows for ages trying to spot the wonderful sight of Blackpool tower, convinced it would appear on the horizon at any moment.

"Bolton terminus," shouted the driver, and his clippie assistant indicated that we should all get off at once. We scrambled down to find ourselves in the centre of a very busy roundabout, traffic hurtling in every direction and no signpost to the beach anywhere! Confused, and by now a little unsettled, we asked a passing lady if we were anywhere near Blackpool. She smiled kindly and told us that no, sadly, Blackpool was still a long way away and asked where we had come from. We explained our journey and she advised us to catch the next bus back to Manchester and then get home before we became hopelessly lost.

These were of course pre-mobile days, and even pre-landline days, so we simply had to take this lady's words seriously. All we knew was we were a long way from home and beginning to feel just a little scared. Under the guidance of this lady, we climbed aboard the returning bus back to the city centre, decidedly hungry and thirsty, the small parcel of sandwiches and bottle of lemonade long gone. The journey returning to Manchester appeared to take forever (approximately 10 miles) and the afternoon was extremely hot. How tired and frightened we suddenly began to feel.

Nonetheless, on alighting from the bus, we spied the trolley bus that had originally carried us into the city centre. Handing over the very last few pennies we had, we cheerfully climbed aboard and almost fell from this trolley when the familiar park came into view. What a relief, and what an adventure. We could tell by our rumbling tummies that it was almost tea time and rushed home agreeing to say nothing of our day at the coast!

Bounding through the door, I rejoiced in the sight and smell of the evening meal about to be served. "Wash your hands and sit down quickly," my mother said. "Where have you been? You were almost late."

Scuttling to wash my hands, I shouted over my shoulder, "Blackpool." Hearing her laugh, I realised that we had not even been missed.

My main companions when small consisted of cousins and three friends who all lived close as neighbours. Two sisters by the name of Miriam and Hazel, and a slightly older girl who lived next door to the sisters called Maureen. Like many small girls, we loved to dress up and put on shows for our parents. As I recall, we had a dressing-up box full of odd items, but mainly old hats. During this time ladies wore hats on a daily basis and so lots of old ones were usually available. The dressing-up box was kept in Maureen's house and, as she was keeper of the clothes and also a year older than the rest of us, she pulled rank when it came to first pick of hats.

I can picture one particular hat to this day, black shiny straw with a purple brim and lots of sparkle over the crown. This hat had the added attraction of smelling wonderfully of what we thought was an exotic perfume, although it was probably *Evening in Paris*. For some reason, we all loved this hat and longed to wear it, but unless Maureen was in a particularly benevolent mood we did not stand a chance.

We lived in terraced houses with rather capacious cellars, great for playing in, but rather cold most of the year. Maureen lived in a jeweller's shop and we loved to go inside after trading hours and look at all the lovely things on display. The shop had a large yard behind it, and in one corner of this yard stood a coal bunker with a huge concrete slab for a cover. It made an excellent stage and many musicals were performed on the concrete slab. However, it all came to a sad end one sunny day when we were performing for our mothers. The last item was Miriam dancing and twirling, until the concrete slab broke in two pieces with a loud crack, hurtling Miriam down between the two and breaking her leg! That was the end of our stage careers, and sadly, the end of Miriam's summer.

One of the most vivid memories of that time had to be the death of Maureen's father, John. He was a kind, gentle man, but he had never enjoyed good health, as I recall, always suffering with chest infections. One sad day, Maureen told us he had died, and then added that we could see him if we wished. Death was very much a part of life then and the deceased would often lie in the house in their coffin until the funeral. John was placed in his coffin on the counter of the jeweller's shop, which seemed the logical place for it to be. They did not after all have a 'parlour' where most coffins would rest. The shop was closed, and so led by Maureen, we filed in to see John resting in peace. Maureen's mum, who loved John dearly, was sitting on a stool by the coffin stroking his hand from time to time.

We three girls gazed at him and marvelled at how calm and well he looked after years of struggling with ill health, his pallor usually extremely pale. It did not appear odd that he should rest there until the funeral, and many neighbours and their children filed past his coffin to say goodbye. How different it all is today, with the deceased segregated from the family and frequently not even seen again. We have, I think, gone too far, often wanting to pretend that death does not even happen.

Living as part of a large family group sometimes led to considerable confusion. There were far too many of us to all get into one house at the same time, though this was rectified by everyone making their way to the park on summer evenings. The entire clan would arrive with blankets, cricket bats, footballs, etcetera, and a good time was had by all. However, it was understood that on specific holidays, such as Christmas, we would spend the day in our individual family groups. Then when Boxing Day came, we would arrive in waves dictated by how many chairs one could squeeze into each house.

One year on the day before Christmas Eve, when I was still quite small, perhaps five years old, my mother was involved in preparations for Christmas day, but without her usual enthusiasm. The turkey was bought and the cake made, but she became slower and slower as the day wore on, eventually declaring that she felt most unwell and would go to bed early, hoping the long rest would revive her in time for the busy day ahead. Christmas Eve dawned and it was bitterly cold. My mother, shivering in bed, realised she was quite incapable of getting out of it. She had the flu, joining hundreds of others in the area, it seemed, just in time for Christmas.

My father, who had risen early and gone off to work, suddenly reappeared grey-faced and shaking. Clearly, he too had the flu and within minutes was also tucked up in bed. This left me in a bit of a dilemma as to what I should do next, but as they both asked for water, I busied myself finding a jug to fill and a couple of glasses to sit on the bedside table.

The day wore on and still they slept, waking only to sip water and ask for more before slipping into a deep sleep again. The kitchen had a bread bin full of bread and I found a box of biscuits. This would have to be my dinner that night. I was not too sad, loving chocolate biscuits, my ideal meal!

Christmas day arrived and I woke early excited at the prospect of Father Christmas having visited whilst I slept. Oh, the shock of discovering he had missed my house completely, not a parcel in sight, and the house was left freezing. I had no idea how to make a fire, this being the days well before central heating, or indeed electric fires, for our household. There was coal in the fireplace but lighting it was a complete mystery as far as I was concerned. Making my way into my parents' bedroom, I found them still poorly and wanting only water yet again. I complained that Father Christmas had not been there and was told that he too had taken to his bed with the flu and would deliver the parcels when he felt better! I was rescued later that day when an aunt appeared to wish us a Happy Christmas, finding me eating chocolate biscuits. Horrified, my aunt Florence asked why I had not gone to her for help, but I remembered everyone saying they would spend Christmas day with their own family and thought I must not intrude. It was a Christmas I would not soon forget and I told anyone who would listen that Father Christmas had caught the flu from my mum and dad!

I spent quite a lot of time in my early pre-school years with my paternal grandmother. Looking back on those days, I thought she was a rather severe character, though on reflection I must admit that after raising six children of her own the very last thing she would have wanted was to look after yet another pre-school child. I learned recently from my older cousin Joan that this amazing lady made all the clothes for her brood of six. She baked hams and pickled herrings to offer for sale in the shop they owned, not to mention put a hot meal on the table twice a day. She was never unkind and treated me well, so well in fact that when I started school at the tender age of four, I would frequently run to my grandmother's home, wanting to be with her instead of at my own home.

Even now, one particular day is etched clearly in my mind. I could only have been four at the most and not yet started school. Grandma told me we would be going to Blackpool for the day with her sister and two of her daughters. This sounded wonderful and we boarded a coach—or charabanc, as they were called in those days—to ride to the coast. Blackpool was, and is still, well known for not only the tower but the splendid pier, its long length packed with exciting things to see and do. We walked the length of the pier and, to my amazement, at the very end found a dance band playing to a crowd of figures ballroom dancing, singing along to all the popular tunes of the day.

My grandma and aunts beamed with delight. After placing me on a bench, they told me to sit still and watch, while off they whirled, leading each other by the waist. At first I was captivated by the sight and sounds, but then the floor began to fill with figures waltzing along and I suddenly realised I could not see my family. Jumping down from the bench, I ran around the whirling figures, but could find no trace of them. Concluding they had left the pier and me, I ran the length of the pier crying loudly. I soon found myself surrounded by a crowd who produced a couple of policemen to sort out my plight. After some time, and the policemen failing to get any sense out of me, they sighed with relief to hear me suddenly yell, "There's my grandmother!" as she and my aunts appeared through the crowd. Unlike today, where I feel I should have been hugged and told all was well, or alternatively told off by an anxious parent, my grandmother simply laughed and yanked me off back to the charabanc.

My cousin Joan was the eldest of my bunch of cousins and she recalls a great deal more about those earlier days with grandma then I do. She reminded me of the fact that no matter how busy she was looking after her large family, she was still smartly turned out. I loved the story she told me about Grandma visiting her home when she was a little girl. As was the fashion in those days, Grandma wore a hat and a fox fur stole. I actually remember the fox fur quite well. The method of construction was to keep the head intact and the four legs dangling from this rather gruesome item. The tongue was replaced by a piece of hard bone, which you could make click realistically. The stole and the hat were given to Joan, who was instructed to take them upstairs and place them gently on one of the beds until it was time for Grandma to leave. With glee, Joan would take the fox stole and tie a piece of string around its neck, pretending it was a dog, and had a wonderful time playing with it—though out of sight!

My maternal grandparents were cut from a very different cloth, not only from my paternal grandparents but from everyone else, it seemed. My grandmother was Irish, with such a strong accent I could never understand a word she said. My grandfather was Welsh and his accent also left me completely clueless. I was quite young when they both died, but I was left with only a memory of complete incomprehension.

These mysterious grandparents had arrived from their rural homeland to Manchester looking for employment, and secured employment in large financially well-heeled households. My grandmother was employed as a maid and my grandfather as a butler. One link that amazes me even today is that my grandfather Isaac came from Anglesey, or Isle of Angels as it is in Welsh, and my other grandfather eventually had business premises in Angel Meadow, Manchester, both places becoming significant in my later life. Sarah and Isaac, my maternal grandparents, lived in the district of Manchester, known as Newton Heath, which to my knowledge had three claims to fame. The first being that it gave rise to the world-famous Manchester United Football team. This team was originally known as Newton Heath L.R.Y. The initials stood for Lancashire and Yorkshire Railway and was formed in 1878 by railway workers, known as The Heathens. I feel the second claim to fame was, unsurprisingly, the large railway works and rolling stock. Trains could be heard all times of day and night, and a major source of employment. The third claim to fame is the fact that Judy Finnigan was born there. I believe she and I were born in the same nursing home, a small homely spot called Beech Mount. Newton Heath was a very poor working class area, but it has produced some sparkling talent.

My mother had two older brothers and a younger sister, all spaced out chronologically because my grandfather served in World War I. They had produced two boys before it began, and the second batch of children didn't emerge until after the war was over. George, my mother's eldest brother, was twelve years her senior, but by the time she entered her teenage years, George was long gone. Gone indeed being the operative word because he left home at age eighteen and was never seen again. He could have been anywhere in the world, we mused, but Mom said they eventually forgot all about him.

Some twenty-five years later, I was looking forward to a day at the seaside with a church group. My mother, a Sunday school teacher in this church, was accompanying her class along with dozens of others on this much-anticipated day out. We assembled at the then main station in Manchester, namely Manchester Central, eagerly waiting on the platform for the time to climb aboard. The huge steam engine came into sight, puffing and making a huge amount of noise—the age of steam. Shuddering to a halt, it awaited the time of departure, the guard shouting, "All aboard!"

Just as we were about to board this huge train, the driver stepped down from his cab to see if all was well. He and my mother locked eyes and stared for a moment before my mum cried out, "It's your Uncle George!"

Indeed it was and they had a little chat before the train had to leave, but George said they would talk more on arrival at the seaside. True to his word, we caught up with him at our destination and he chatted happily to his little sister for the first time in twenty-five years. He did not know his parents had died and appeared to be surprised by that fact. However, not as surprised as my mother when he admitted he'd never left the area, living ten minutes away from his old home while working on the railways. It was a very strange day, and even stranger was the fact that we never saw him again. He vanished into the steam as before, the elusive Uncle George once seen and never forgotten!

TAKE IN A SHOW

Sunday afternoons feature prominently in my early memories. We always attended chapel and we always had ice cream for dessert following Sunday afternoon tea. The ice cream in question was purchased from the legendary *Gotteli's* ice cream parlour—which, you will be surprised to learn, was owned and run by an Italian family. The premises included a parlour where people might sit and drink herbal delights, this being an alcohol-free zone. The counter where the ice cream was sold was a long narrow corridor, always full of people waiting to be served.

The custom was to arrive with a suitable receptacle—in my case a glass jug—and it would be filled with as many scoops as you might require, then delicious raspberry sauce poured over them. Afterwards, you tried to run home before they melted. Reaching my early teens, I would accompany a group of friends (my good chum Joan in particular) to the splendid sounding park known as Boggart Hole Clough—which actually is still popular to this day.

We played 'pitch and putt' for some time until finally filling the booths in *Gotteli's* for glasses of hot Vimto. How sophisticated life was in those days! However, Sunday afternoon remains significant for one other reason, the chorus girls. We lived only a few streets away from a hugely popular establishment known as The Hippodrome. Each week the cast of this palace of delights would move on and the company for the following week would arrive. Without fail, several chorus girls would knock on the door asking for lodgings and, without fail, we had to decline. My parents felt sorry for these young girls, who always looked so cold, pinched of face and hungry, but we simply did not have the space to accommodate them. Shows at the Hippodrome were of the old-fashioned variety and would feature well-known singers of the day, magicians and comedians. Huge crowds would flock nightly to these shows, but then it was pre-television in those days.

My grandmother and friends took to attending the afternoon matinee of these shows, and particularly enjoyed the sing-along sessions. If the show was suitable, occasionally I would be allowed to go with them. Often in the run-up to Christmas there would be a pantomime to see.

My grandfather had a shop of many delights which featured a section selling groceries, whilst another room had booths, this being an 'outdoor beer licence' where people could sit and drink. After the nightly show at the Hippodrome many of the cast and crew would arrive at my grandfather's shop for a well-earned drink. Many of the unknown comics and singers would go on to be household names, and I was told even Charlie Chaplin had once been welcomed for a drink. I have been told, and have no reason to doubt, that Charlie Chaplin started his career as a tap dancer with a group known as the *Eight Lancashire Lads*, but moved on to being a comedian on the Vaudeville circuit where at the turn of the century he found himself performing at the Hippodrome. He was still very young then, long before he travelled to the U.S. with his Vaudeville acts, but then as they say, the rest is history.

Hearing about all the excitement of this palace of delight, my mother, a sweet but rather naive lady, decided she would treat her Sunday school class to an evening at the Hippodrome. I had told her about the pantomimes my grandmother had taken me to and how jolly some of the afternoon performances had been—where we would sing to all the tunes of the day. Christmas was approaching and so my mother went along to ask what the festive season feature would be. She was told the show would be called *Jane in Snow Land.* She thought this would be lovely for her class of little girls and bought tickets for a matinee show. To my delight, I was included in this outing and so looked forward to the Christmas special.

The appointed afternoon arrived and we all jostled with the crowds to get into the auditorium. Oddly enough, there did not appear to be any other children and my mother was receiving strange looks from people in the crowd queuing to go inside. I was very young, but still recall the entrance was filled with imitation trees draped with snow and a large poster of a lady in a woolly hat and scarf draped with what appeared to be a red curtain. It all looked very odd, but we pressed on. After finding our seats, we waited for the lights to go down and the curtain to go up.

On came the chorus girls singing about snow and wonderland and all appeared well. Suddenly the curtain came down and there was a hushed silence of anticipation, until it rose once more to reveal naked ladies, with one particularly voluptuous blonde centre stage wearing nothing but a woolly hat!

This was Jane and the show was an erotic take on winter.

In those days women could appear nude as long as they did not move. Clearly this show would be a series of tableaux featuring Jane standing silently amid the winter snow. Shocked to her core, my poor mother, with a red face and great speed, ushered her Sunday school class out of the place as fast as their little legs would allow. I do not know how all was explained to their parents, but I doubt my mother ever again entered the Hippodrome!

My friends and I however, especially Joan and her brothers, who lived close to this wonderful place, realised that all was not totally wholesome about the Vaudeville shows, and they eventually discovered that the large double doors at the rear of the building did not close tightly. These would be opened at the end of the show to allow extra exits and appeared to be only loosely joined together. If several of us leaned simultaneously on these double doors they would gape sufficiently for a couple of kids at a time to peer inside. Joan, and especially her brothers, would be particularly valuable for this task.

This then was the method by which I saw many shows growing up, widening my education and answering many questions I could not possibly have asked my parents. My friends were a diverse group attending different junior schools and places of worship. Several of these close friends happened to be of the Roman Catholic faith, but I do not recall any problems arising from this fact. The large Catholic Church was called St. Edmunds and amongst other attractions for small boys it had a pipe band. Manchester at this time had a strong tradition of Whitsun Walks, which involved the different denominations parading with bands and banners on different days for the duration of Whit Week. Church of England parishes would parade on the Monday, Catholic Churches on the Friday, followed by the non-conformists the following Sunday. Finally, on Sunday evenings, there would be a colourful parade of people from Poland and the Ukraine, plus Italians. It was a busy week and exciting time for participants.

Attending all these marches and parades was an experience much anticipated by all. My friends had a particular attraction for the St. Edmunds Parade due to the fact that the leader of the pipe band was a much-admired, handsome chap who we thought looked splendid in a kilt. He would throw his baton in the air, twirling it as he did so, and catch it faultlessly. He was a smart and rather kind lad called Brian Cashinella, who had an ambition to become a journalist.

Often our little group, after riding bikes or a game of cricket, would walk home together, and Brian, being such a kind, thoughtful boy, was everyone's favourite companion.

Brian would keep the peace amongst our group, ensuring that there was never any bullying or unkindness to the girls. In our late teens several of the group left for pastures new, I for Los Angeles and Brian for the bright lights of Fleet Street. Decades later I came across him at the B.B.C. where he had been interviewed about his very successful career as a journalist on national and international newspapers. He was now the much-admired journalist and crime writer Brian Cashinella. Our little group (that had dispersed world-wide to the United States, Canada, Australia and South America, just to name a few countries) had become experts in many fields. Indeed a cousin of mine had a wonderful career in the army, and one of my youngest cousins became a world expert and professional mountain climber, as indeed he still is today.

LEAVING MANCHESTER AT LAST

My very first taste of the 'outside world' came in the last year of junior school. The top class, as we were called, had been invited to attend the Festival of Britain in London. The idea of seeing London was so exciting that I could scarcely wait to run home and ask permission from my parents. The cost was minimal due to the fact that many concessions for school children were readily available: train tickets, entrance tickets, etcetera, and so, to my delight, my parents agreed to let me go.

This wonderful event was to take place in the summer of 1951 and the whole concept was to cheer everyone after the dark days of the second World War. At this time, having fairly recently witnessed the end of hostilities, much of London was still in ruins and desperately in need of redevelopment. It was to be the tonic everyone needed to get the country back on its feet. In class, we were told about some of the exciting things we should be able to see, and although most appeared to be beyond comprehension, they nevertheless sounded most exciting.

Getting there would be an adventure in itself. The very concept of going to London by train appeared quite wonderful, though it exceeded even our wildest dreams. We found excitement not only in placing our small suitcases (we stayed only two nights) in the racks, but smelling the steam from the train, and we were fascinated by all the people. With great interest, we walked down the train corridor looking at the other passengers. I suddenly noticed one of my favourite English film stars sitting in a carriage with his wife, whom I also instantly recognised, the very lovable Peter Butterworth and Janet Brown. I had in fact seen Peter Butterworth in films that year, this before we had a television set. Eventually, however, my kindly grandmother bought each family member a television set, enabling us to watch the coronation of Elizabeth the second.

Before this exciting event it had been traditional for my parents (along with many of our neighbours) to take me along to the local cinema on a weekly basis to see the latest film offered. In the future, I would watch Peter Butterworth on television for many years. However, I digress. At that moment on the train, I saw my very first celebrity. Thrilled out of any form of shyness, I instantly went to speak to them. I am happy to report they were simply lovely and chatted away to me, even signing a ticket I had placed in my pocket. On reflection, returning home, I thought this was perhaps the most exciting part of the trip.

Arriving in the capital late in the afternoon we marched along in a crocodile to eat our evening meal. I cannot for the life of me remember, or even imagine, where this might have been, but the next stage of the trip is indelibly etched in my mind. We were led down many stone steps to an old underground station, where row upon row of camp beds were arranged, each with pillows and blankets. There was a wash area and toilets, the whole thing quite astonishing to our eyes. I can only assume that this had been in use as a shelter during the bombing raids, and not yet been returned to the underground system.

It cannot have been too cold because this was May and the day had indeed been very hot. We were all quite tired at this point and readily fell asleep, but I woke wondering where on earth I was and could this be a dream. It was clearly very early morning when we left the station, because as we exited into the sunshine above, the streets were all but deserted. I can still see in my mind's eye the surreal thrill of walking through Trafalgar Square and seeing those familiar lions in the early-morning sunshine.

At one point, we found a bus awaiting us and we climbed aboard to drive down Whitehall to see the Houses of Parliament. Across the river, we went to the South Bank and had breakfast somewhere near the site, but again I could not swear to the exact location. When it came time to enter the Festival of Britain, I recall we were amongst the first that day to go inside and see the amazing sights.

I was still young and memory fails in some areas of detail, but I do have vivid memories of certain installations. Shining in the sunlight, the famous Skylon was a giant silver cigar balancing on a tiny base above the ground. It appeared to hang in mid-air, defying gravity. I thought it amazing. There were lots of halls and buildings containing exhibitions of various kinds. A large Pleasure park was available for us to eat our lunch, as well as to let off a little steam.

One more vivid memory lingers for me and that was an area depicting farming. It was a huge space with lots of bales of hay in every direction. I recall my teachers' panic as the boys from my class ran headlong at the bales of hay. The boys especially were climbing with gusto everywhere, swarming like ants and disappearing into the crowd. How brave those teachers must have been to take a class of thirty school children to London and let them loose in a huge theme park. Somehow we all managed to reconvene and get back to Manchester unscathed. It whetted my appetite to see more of the capital, and to this day I never cease to feel a thrill of expectation arriving by train in London—despite having done this countless times during my life.

QUITE A FEAST

Shortly after this wonderful adventure to London, we were informed that our lovely junior school headmistress was retiring. I wondered if the Festival of Britain expedition had seen her off because it had been so stressful. Bless her, she announced she would leave at the end of the summer term. Apparently, this spinster by the name of Miss Woodfine had always held a dream in her heart that one day she would retire to a secluded spot in Wales, and at last her dream was about to become reality.

Chatting with my mother one day, she revealed that she had purchased a remote cottage deep in rural Wales and was looking forward to a lot of peaceful days ahead. Discussing this later that same evening, my parents expressed concern that she might be lonely there all by herself, especially as she had revealed there would be no immediate neighbours in this new location. The last day of term arrived and the school presented lovely Miss Woodfine with gifts and many good wishes for her new life so far away from busy inner Manchester. Many tears were shed as she left the school building for the last time. My parents informed her that we would often take holidays in North Wales and she pressed for our address, entreating them to call should they be in the vicinity. She appeared to be so genuine in this request and my parents worried for her welfare. The very next summer we wrote to her and arranged to visit.

We usually stayed in a very small hotel by the coast, rather quaint, but homely, and the home cooking superb. On the designated evening of our visit to see Miss Woodfine, the kind lady of the hotel suggested we eat an early evening meal to give us plenty of time to drive to the cottage. The evening was warm and sunny. At the end of June dusk does not arrive until quite late in the U.K.

Having enjoyed a wonderful early meal of baked ham, meat pies, salads, delicious homemade bread and various desserts, we prepared to drive to the cottage. Fortunately, my father was familiar with North Wales and did not predict any problems in finding the good lady's home. We were full and happy, looking forward to spending the evening reunited with the dear Miss Woodfine.

Years later when I came across a copy of *Mrs. Pepperpot,* I realised that our dear old headmistress could well have been the inspiration behind the illustrations. Small, round and twinkly with her hair in a bun, she was cute and extremely friendly. After only a slight hiccup at the very end of our drive, we found the remote cottage. It was a chocolate box painting, so very pretty with a wonderful garden, colourful and scent-filled. Knocking on the door we all felt an air of excited expectation.

Opening the door, the lovely little lady chuckled with delight and gave us all a welcoming hug. "You are exactly on time," she said. "Come inside, everything is ready."

Rather confused, we looked at each as to what was 'ready' but followed her indoors at once. She led us through the pretty little lounge to the dining room, where she had prepared a huge spread! "Sit down and begin at once," she declared. "I am sure you must be hungry after your drive."

The table was groaning under the weight of home baked ham, meat pies, salads, homemade bread and various desserts. Oh my, what a pickle we were in (and yes, plenty of those on the table too)! Sitting down at the table, we stared at each other at a loss as to what we should do. Miss Woodfine went into the kitchen to brew a pot of tea and my mother hissed, "Under the circumstances, we should just do the best we can."

That night I simply could not sleep due to a tummy ache. The next morning, we all declined breakfast—and, as I recall, did not recover for quite some time!

MY KINGDOM FOR A HORSE!

It might have been the memory of that gargantuan supper in Wales, but the following year my parents decided we should visit a new location for our holiday. I was never keen on holidays, (being an only child coupled with my parents' preference for quiet spots) as they always left me lonely and bored. I would, however, miss the trips to the cinema, which always happened at least twice when we had stayed in a rented cottage on Anglesey. The tiny cinema was filled every night with holiday makers. Not only was there a great film to see each night, but they had an interval where tea and biscuits would be served, passing the cups of tea down the rows of people.

My spirits were raised at the thought of not holidaying in quiet North Wales, looking forward to our new holiday destination at Knott End. Unfortunately, this turned out to be the sort of place where absolutely nothing happened. Later in life, someone remarked to me that if you stood there for an hour or so, bugger all happened. There was little beach to speak of and save for a small grocer, there did not appear to be any shops. The only saving grace was a small ferry that took you across to the seaside town of Fleetwood and, in desperation, we did this several times a day.

You may think that today this would have blossomed into a thriving seaside location with many shops and cafes to enjoy. You would, however, be wrong. There is still bugger-all happening there.

On arrival in this buzzing metropolis, we emptied our car and followed a rather solemn-looking lady upstairs to our bedrooms. *It is going to be a long week*, I thought. *Here we go again, another dead-end town.*

Later in the afternoon, I was distinctly cheered as the front door opened and in breezed a girl perhaps a couple of years older than myself. "This is my daughter, Lizzy," said the solemn-faced woman. "She has been riding her horse." Turning to my parents, she added, "Perhaps your daughter would like a ride. Lizzy would be happy to take her."

"That would be splendid," my mother agreed. Even though I had never been within spitting distance of a horse in my life, I thought it might be a jolly diversion.

The following afternoon, Lizzy announced that we would go to the stables where her horse 'Betsy' would be waiting for us. As soon as we left the house, Lizzy gave me a firm dig in my back and said, "Don't get the idea we are friends, and don't think we are doing this more than once." She glowered at me and ran ahead without waiting for me to catch up.

I had not a clue as to what I should do or say to this onslaught, but followed as quickly as I could. We soon reached a large field with a small stable in one corner. Lizzy disappeared into the stable and came out leading the biggest horse I had ever seen. "I don't suppose you can ride?" this sullen girl asked. When I said indeed I could not, she then pulled the horse to the eight-bar gate. "Climb the gate and put your leg over the horse and sit in the saddle," she instructed. I did as I was told, completely petrified, but desperate that she should not know this. But Lizzy was, if nothing else, canny and she knew full well the horse scared me to death. "Hold on to the reins," she instructed and slowly led the horse across an absolutely huge field.

At this point, I was in fact thinking that this was quite pleasant. We moved at such a slow, steady pace and I felt reassured, even though the horse was huge and the ground a long way down. We stopped in the very centre of this large field and Betsy put her head down and immediately began to eat the grass. Lizzy let go of the reins and ran as fast as she could back the way we had come, laughing hysterically at my predicament. Soon she was out of sight, leaving me sitting on top of this gigantic horse, apparently munching away on the grass with no thought of me on her back.

The horse was too tall and I could not get down, nor could I reach the reins, which Lizzy had dropped over the horse's head, and I was a long way from the eight-bar gate. Well, there was nothing for it but to sit still and hope the minx came back for me—she did not! I sat on this gentle giant for better part of half an hour, dusk falling when a gentleman (who, it transpired, actually owned the field) suddenly arrived.

I shouted for help and he strode towards me purposefully. "What are you doing on Lizzy's horse?" he demanded. When I related the incident, he clearly struggled to keep a straight face. He coughed loudly and took the reins, walking Betsy back to the edge of the field, where he then, thankfully, helped me down. My legs hurt and I felt a fool, but I was determined not to cry, especially as I had no idea how to get back to the hotel. However, my rescuer directed me and I began to walk back, ruminating on what I might say. There was no sign of the evil Lizzy, and in fact, she did not appear until much later, after the evening meal.

Suddenly she popped her head around the door, grinning. "Did you enjoy your ride on my horse?"

"Oh, yes!" I replied. "Shortly after getting used to the saddle, I found riding was quite easy and we had a lovely time galloping around the field." I smiled beatifically at her confused, and now thunderous, face. But I had learned my lesson, I *never* wanted to be on the back of another horse, not for the rest of my life.

DON'T PUT YOUR DAUGHTER ON THE STAGE

In my mid-teens, still California dreaming, it occurred to me that maybe I should get some acting experience under my belt. After all, there was a strong possibility that, along with many other stars, I might be spotted in *Schwabs* drugstore on Sunset Boulevard. Considering I did indeed bear a strong resemblance to Veronica Lake, this new venture would require some preparation.

To my amazement and delight, sometime later I actually made it to Schwabs—an amazing place which sadly was bulldozed in 1983.

For my immediate plan, I decided to join an amateur dramatic group in the centre of Manchester and went along with high expectations. I might not be offered the lead female role the first time I auditioned but surely it would not be long before my talent became obvious. After all, I had taken part in every panto mime my little chapel had produced, and even the odd play!

Not without difficulty, I found the building for this group, hidden away as it was under the railway arches of the city. It looked a little dingy from the outside, but they had indeed made a splendid job of creating a small intimate theatre inside. There was a rehearsal taking place as I arrived for their next production, which was to be "Sweet Bird of Youth." This really impressed me because I was a great fan of Tennessee

Williams. Chatting to the producer, I informed him that I should very much like to join the company. He instructed me to turn up bright and early the following Saturday afternoon and he would tell me where I might start.

Saturday dawned and, with mounting excitement, I made my way to the theatre in the early afternoon. People were dashing around, sorting out costumes etcetera, and on spotting me, the producer said, "Ah, yes, report to the makeup room for instructions."

A smiling lady welcomed me, and said my first job would be to apply fake tan to the leading man. This was a time long before spray tans had been thought of. Apparently, a layer of tan had to be applied each night by hand with a sponge to this young chap, I was a little disappointed at being handed such a lowly task, but when the gorgeous young man appeared to have his torso covered in tan, I found myself warming to the task.

Well, I pondered, *I suppose I should start his tan at the bottom—well, not the bottom exactly, but the lower torso!*

As the week, and several performances, went by, I found myself looking forward to being a fake-tan applicator. Eventually the last night arrived, clearly a successful production, and I was invited to the after-show party. I loved every moment of it, sure at the time that I was clearly meant for the show biz lifestyle.

Soon after, a decision was made about the following production. The producer informed me that I should be in charge of props. *Oh, my,* I thought, *they clearly think I need to learn every aspect of production.* So, I resigned myself to this new area of show business, though distinctly cheered to learn another girl would be helping me. I instantly liked Karen, a jolly, friendly girl, and unexpectedly Australian. This next play would need a great many props, though the most important part of our job was to play the sound of a motorcycle at the correct moment during the performance. This was a big responsibility and had to be spot on cue or we would ruin the entire production.

We were given a tape recorder and told to listen carefully to the actors. A rather daunting aspect of this was the fact that we had to sit on top of a rack-like structure suspended just above the stage overlooking the actors. It was a little wobbly, which gave cause for concern, not to mention the fact that Karen and I were decidedly giggly, and the giggling made this structure swing alarmingly. Still, we managed to complete several rehearsals without mishap.

The first night arrived and the house was full. It was time for us to climb aboard our lofty perch, ready for action. At this point, Karen appeared with two pint pots of beer, one for each of us. Even though I insisted I had never tasted the stuff before, she persuaded me to try one. Well, I cannot say I particularly liked the taste of beer, but I felt a wimp not to give it a whirl. To my surprise, it soon went down rather well. We managed our motorbike sound effects perfectly well, finding it all rather good fun sitting above the action.

After the interval, I once more prepared to sit astride this rather uncomfortable platform, when Karen appeared with two more pint pots of beer. This time I did not protest and Karen said I should soon grow to like the taste. Apparently, she had been weaned on the stuff! Sipping away, I soon found my giggles growing beyond my control, and rather loud stage whispers of "Shush!" began to reach us from below. All this did was tickle us even further and our giggles soon turned to laughter. The moment arrived when the motorbike noise should be deployed, but the rack we were sitting had begun to swing erratically. Reaching out to steady the rack, and switch on the recorder, I somehow managed to knock my full pint of beer off the rack right onto the head of the leading man standing centre stage below. He yelled with rage, the audience howled with laughter, and we both fell off the swinging rack onto the stage in a heap of giggles!

My career as an actress ended as quickly as the curtain was drawn across the stage. I beat a hasty retreat from the theatre, never to return.

Over the years, I have visited Los Angeles many times for many different reasons. I would visit old friends, acquire new ones, and undertake work in various capacities. I have enjoyed taking my two daughters to visit my old haunts in this exciting city. Val produced three strapping boys, all six-foot-plus and we would exchange children in the long summer holidays. It was great fun to have her boys visit, even though they positively filled the place.

I'm sure the boys found a small Lancashire town very quaint after the large city of Los Angeles, but they nevertheless appeared to enjoy their trips to England. Perhaps it is unsurprising due to their location, but all three eventually had input with the world of show business. Christopher, the eldest, became a musician, while Dominic became an actor, and the youngest Anthony, a very successful script writer and director.

A rather funny sequel to this tale happened when Anthony found himself in a meeting with producers and directors in Hollywood, one of whom happened to be the now famous Danny Boyle. During a coffee break, Anthony asked Danny whereabouts in England he had come from. Danny smiled and said, "Oh, you will not have heard of it, a very small town in Lancashire called Radcliffe."

Anthony chuckled and replied, "Not only have I heard of it, I have visited there many times. My aunt lives there."

The entire room was astonished, not least of all Danny Boyle. As you will have guessed, Val is honorary aunt to my girls, as I am to her boys, and it was in fact only when they were grown that the boys discovered that I was not a real aunt.

At this point, I must tell you that my little charge Robbie also grew up to be a famous writer in Hollywood. Amongst others, he was a writer for the television show "Frasier," humour inherited from Arthur obviously in his genes, one of the funniest men I have ever known.

On one glorious occasion while visiting Los Angeles with my daughter Rachel, a grown Rob, as he is now called, arranged for us to go onto the set of Frazier to watch a rehearsal. Accompanied by August and Val, we went along one evening with great excitement. Frasier was hugely popular and it was wonderful to see all the famous actors screening their latest episode at such close quarters. We were even introduced to the wee dog Eddie and amazed to discover that the actor John Mahoney, who played the father in the show, was in fact originally a Mancunian!

SYNCHRONICITY

Over my life, I have found many of my closest friends have appeared during unusual circumstances or by coincidence, my good friend Gary Quinn no exception. Gary and I met in London many years ago, forming an instant bond. He is an intuitive life coach in Los Angeles, a best-selling author, and international television and radio star, just to list a few of his attributes. On top of all that, he is great fun and a joy to spend time with.

We decided fairly early in our friendship that we would collaborate in many areas—and have done so ever since, in the United Kingdom, United States and many other European countries. We co-wrote several books leading to many broadcasting appointments, which proved to be extremely enjoyable. All these wonderful times have led to fascinating encounters.

Our first joint television interview saw us on the flagship programme "This Morning" with fellow guests Peter Kaye and Michael Flatley. Both these men were charming, but Peter's career was in its infancy and, despite coming from the same corner of northern England, I did not know who he was. We were fortunate enough to be guests on the programme many times both together, as well as separately. These were the days of Fern Brittan and Peter Schofield, both delightful presenters and very kind to guests. Fern is one of the nicest people one could ever have the pleasure of meeting. Later, when I became involved as a writer for magazines, he was more than happy to give me interviews.

My first experience at *'going live'* was after the publication of my first book back in 1996. This book too came to fruition because of amazing synchronicity, leading me to my wonderful editor Judith Kendra of Random House. Judith found me completely by accident and thus began a working, friendly relationship which was to last for many years. With the publicity department at the publishers introducing me to the world of media, I found myself a guest on radio shows, instantly finding this a medium I absolutely adored.

One of my first radio interviews happened to be with the now ITV morning contributor Richard Arnold, who at that time had his own show for Liberty Radio. We had such fun and enjoyed the experience so much that I was invited to be a guest whenever I found myself in London, which happened fairly often over the next couple of years. Almost all local BBC radio stations invited me as a guest, and eventually this led to television. Much to my delight, I found myself a fairly regular guest of "This Morning."

One morning I arrived bright and early as usual, but when the time came for makeup to be applied I was told that my top was unsuitable and would cause the camera to *strobe*, not a desired effect. I was instructed to go to the wardrobe department and find another top to wear for the show. There were rows and rows of items to choose from, but the wardrobe lady found one she considered suitable, as well as flattering. It was, dear readers, bright gold, very blingy, and not at all a subdued hue. In addition, I was festooned with a pair of gold earrings to complete the picture. At this point, my makeup lady decided to take it on as a challenge and proceeded to give me some fairly heavy makeup to compete with the gold. Looking in the mirror, I scarcely recognised myself, but everyone, including Fern, told me it was a good look.

The show went really well that morning and, as usual, I enjoyed it hugely, and we appeared to reach the end of the morning show in record time. Arriving back at the Green room, I was suddenly confronted by an anxious young man who said my car was waiting to take me back to Euston and, since it was a busy morning with lots of people wanting cars, they would appreciate my going at once. I obliged, grabbing my handbag and light jacket, and was immediately whisked off to Euston station. The day was growing hotter so I stuffed my jacket into my bag and gratefully sank into my seat on the train for the return journey.

Shortly out of London, a lady clearly making her way to the buffet car gave me a huge smile. How sweet, I thought, and smiled in return. This was repeated by several different passengers of both sexes and I could not understand why everyone was so very smiley that morning. As we approached Manchester, I decided to visit the loo, shocked when I caught sight of myself in the mirror. No wonder everyone had been smiling, I looked like Danny La Rue in drag! In the rush to jump into the car, I had forgotten the sparkly gold outfit and the very heavy makeup. Using a tissue as best I could, I began to remove as much of the face paint as possible, but it was a relief to finally arrive home so I could remove the bling!

I loved to be a part of the programme "This Morning" and would eagerly await each invitation, certain that it would be most enjoyable. Many stars would be a revelation, either for their down-to-earth attitude and friendly manner, or occasionally their frosty attitude. I recall one hugely popular "soap star" who shall remain nameless, who refused to sit in the green room with all the other guests. She would remain in her private dressing room until the last minute, having her makeup done in this room as well as served any breakfast treats and coffee.

Most of the guests, and indeed the presenters, would gather in the green room before going on air. Fern would have her makeup and hair attended too along with everyone else so they could take their coffee and chat. I met some lovely people this way, but I do recall one morning in particular, while waiting to be called from the green room. I had been sitting alone with Jenny Bond, the BBC Royal correspondent for many years. She was delightful, friendly, charming and tiny! At one point, she asked very sweetly if she should know who I was. I was tempted to say I was a minor royal she had yet to meet, but decided to answer truthfully, that no indeed she should not know me. I was a mere author waiting to be interviewed about my latest book. She laughed, said she was happy to meet me, and should we attack the Danish pastries and coffee sitting on the table. We helped ourselves and I marvelled at how slight and sylph-like she was, but still completely *real* when it came to enjoying food. In the future, I would compare this with similar situations in Hollywood, of which I'll give more on later.

NEARLY FAMOUS!

My television career almost blossomed at one point. Instead of being the occasional guest on various programmes, the day arrived when I became a semi-permanent fixture. I had been invited for an interview on a jolly programme for ITV Manchester. This afternoon show ran five days a week and featured a different topic each day: sports, cookery, health and beauty and gardening. Then, on a Friday afternoon, it gloried into the title of psychic live time!

Many areas of the paranormal were delved into, from medium ship to dream interpretation. I had recently published a book about synchronicity, featuring spiritual synchronicity, and so I had been invited onto the programme to discuss this. I was interviewed by the lovely Beccy Want (a familiar face to me, having been interviewed several times on her radio show). The whole experience was delightful and interesting, so imagine my joy when I was once more issued with an invitation for the Friday show.

Before long, Friday became a fairly regular delight. I lived within thirty minutes of the studio, a fast car whisking me there once a month or so. It seemed I had progressed from synchronicity to various subject of my choice, a very happy situation indeed. The green room always contained a superb spread of goodies and drinks and the cast became like a family.

We continued in this way for perhaps eighteen months, until one day I was told that the programme would finish for the summer. When it returned in the autumn, I would be offered a permanent Friday afternoon slot. I was thrilled beyond words, especially as they intimated that I could talk about anything I thought might interest the viewers in this field. I had been delving into the effects of colour in our lives, symbolism in nature, and pagan practices and how they impacted on modern day religion. Everyone appeared to be very happy with my suggestions. They told me I would have at least ten minutes to myself on the show every Friday, my cup runneth over!

I spent the summer happily researching subjects of interest while I waited with bated breath for the end of August, the time arranged for me to have a meeting with the powers- that-be. Well, I did get the call at the end of August and it transpired that the powers-that-be, who resided in London, had visited the Manchester studio with grim news. It appeared that viewing figures indicated that Friday psychic live time had wonderful viewing figures, but as the year progressed the other subjects for the rest of the week had fallen considerably. Because of it, they decided to pull the plug and cancel the programme altogether.

It was devastating news for everyone concerned, and our lovely TV family would have to be dispersed far and wide. The wonderful Beccy Want moved to BBC radio full time, where she still has a hugely successful career. Others, however, felt at a loss as to what they might do next. My live television career was over almost before it began, but it had still been an amazing experience and I loved every moment, feeling blessed to have had the experience at all.

Happy days!

To this day, Gary and I often look back with interest and amusement at some of our previous activities. Approximately eight years ago, I joined Gary in California for a tour, which would include workshops and speaking engagements. Many of these events would be in Los Angeles and several more in San Diego. We also had appointments for P.R. involvements and radio and recoding events, not to mention the odd, very odd, party!

We headed first for San Diego, where Gary has a branch of his college. The evening was lovely and well attended, and I was to have a brief speaking spot, but the main lecture was all about positivity and tapping into universal energies. Gary told his audience that if they thought hard enough and put their desires out there, the universe would pick it up and deliver. Not easy, you might think, and indeed many listening thought so too. However, Gary soon had a chance to demonstrate exactly what he was talking about. At the back of the room a man raised his hand and said he was struggling to make ends meet. He had a small apartment, but few possessions. The one thing he desperately needed in the heat of California was a fridge/freezer and how did he suppose he might acquire that by positive thought alone?

Gary smiled and asked the audience, "Does anyone here have a spare fridge/freezer?"

An unlikely request by any standards, but a chap in the front row said, "Yes indeed, I have a spare one. Just bought a new one yesterday and the old one is standing in the garage. He is welcome to it."

I am not sure who was the most surprised, the chap in need, the chap supplying, or the audience. Gary simply smiled again and said, "That is how it all works!"

The following evening, we were to give a joint talk at the world famous Bodhi Tree Book store in Hollywood. This is situated on the famous Melrose Avenue and was an institution in Hollywood. It very sadly closed after more than forty years in 2011, a very grim day indeed. It began in July 1970 in what was then a quiet neighbourhood. The name came from the 'Tree of Enlightenment' under which Gautama sat in meditation. Behind the book store grew a Ficus Religosa Bohdi tree, donated in the early days. It grew nearly three stories high, giving shade for the staff to rest and meet. This was to be a shining light for spiritual books of all descriptions not readily available in those days. This amazing place offered almost daily workshops and lectures and was hugely popular and successful. It turned out to be life-changing for many people just wandering into this place, as Shirley MacLaine revealed in her book "Out on a Limb." As you can possibly imagine, I was thrilled and privileged to be able to speak at this historic store. I now realise how fortunate I was to be there before it sadly had to close.

With this wonderful evening under our belts, Gary and I parted ways to prepare for the next day, for which the schedule made me go pale. Meeting early the next morning in Hollywood, we went first to have publicity photographs taken. These were to be shot by the famous Ute Vile, a truly lovely lady and a good friend of Gary's. It was quite an experience, not to mention a shock at how good she could make unpromising material look.

The next stop of the day was to a television studio, where Gary was to have an interview. it was fascinating to be tagging along and we once more met some super people. Our next port of call was a radio recording studio where we were booked in to record a meditation DVD. While waiting for our studio to become available, Gary spotted a friend about to leave. I thought she looked familiar, and this lovely, and friendly, lady turned out to be Brooke Shields, who had been recoding her book. Our turn came next and I thoroughly enjoyed the experience of recording our DVD.

After a busy morning, we went to meet friends for lunch before heading for the Oscar venue. I kid you not, we got there just as the finishing touches were being put in place for the Oscar ceremony two days hence. Here's the thing, all the glamorous nominees are presented with a goodie bag to take home at the end of the night. I was astonished by the items in these goodie bags, and our involvement was to add to these a copy of Gary's latest book, one proving to be hugely popular, "Living in the Spiritual Zone." On the previous day, the press had published a photograph of Paris Hilton reading a copy! This finished, we had a lovely look around the venue. On leaving, we walked down the steps where the red carpet would soon be placed.

More interviews followed and suddenly it was evening. Gary had informed me that we would be attending a party that night celebrating the opening of a jazz club in Hollywood. I realised with horror that I would not have time to return to the home of my wonderful L.A. Greenberg family, with whom I was staying, to change into something more suitable. In a panic, I dashed into a nearby store and bought a jacket, hoping to uplift my working outfit. I changed in the Ladies room, slapping more makeup on my face and thanked my lucky stars that our lovely photographer had put a thick layer on earlier in the day.

Gary was to collect his good friend Dyan Cannon to take to this event. She had agreed that I might tag along and the lovely lady was so very charming, and a well-known actress in her own right, though equally famous for marrying Cary Grant. She looked amazing and off we went to the jazz club. Arriving was quite an experience, a small taste of what it might be like to live with a celebrity. As we pulled up, a crowd of photographers rushed to the car, flash bulbs popping and questions hurled at Dyan, who, like the trooper she was, calmly took it all in stride.

There were so many famous people in attendance, quite bewildering, stars, directors and producers, and the press was everywhere, asking questions and taking photographs. The new jazz club looked wonderful, live jazz being played all the time. Dyan, bless her, took me by the hand an introduced me to a very well-known film producer and, with a twinkle in her eye, said, "This is Glennyce, from England, but you know of her, of course."

Not to be wrong-footed, the chap said, "Yes, of course I do. Hello, Glennyce." Turning, he said to the next man, "Tis my friend Glennyce from England." It went on and on around the room, the modern-day version of the Emperor's new clothes! Giggling with Gary, we enjoyed every moment.

There was a wonderful buffet of mouth-watering food, but no one was taking a morsel. I was so hungry I would have eaten the piano, but I dared not go and tuck in by myself. Believe it or not, as the evening wore on, nobody ate a thing. I discovered this is how they all stayed so slim and glamorous in Hollywood, but I was starving. It was at this point I remembered Jenny Bond, on the chat show mornings, and how different the attitude was in England to attractive food.

The jazz club was well and truly opened, so Gary, Dyan and myself whisked ourselves away to a late-night film premier. I must confess to struggling to stay awake during the film, but perked up immediately afterwards when we were led outside to a marquee filled with tables of yet more wonderful food. You will probably guess what happened next—no one ate a thing!

Oh my, I thought, *this is not the glamorous film life I had envisaged.* I arrived home in the early hours of the morning and made a beeline for Audrey's kitchen, where I devoured a cheese sandwich. What a day it had been, exhausting and great fun. But guess what, I had to hit the hay because there was another busy day ahead tomorrow!

There was a funny sequel to all the activity of the previous evening however. One day after returning home to Manchester, a magazine arrived in the post from Gary. It was a Hollywood gossip magazine featuring events and goings on in tinsel town. The middle page spread was the "diary page" and there in the middle of all the Hollywood crowd was a picture of Gary and I at the jazz club party with the caption "Gary Quinn and the famous English star Glennyce Eckersley at the club opening!" I rang Gary and we laughed fit to burst. "When you discover what I am famous for, let me know," I said.

There had been only one sad moment regarding my last trip to Los Angeles. Gary had a good friend, Esther Williams. You may well have heard the name. Growing up, she had been an idol of mine: she had of course been an award-winning swimming star. As a child, I had always loved swimming, and my second great love was visiting the cinema, therefore you can probably guess how I adored Esther Williams' wonderful films. My all-time favourite was *Dangerous When Wet.* Her beauty and skill filled me with admiration. Imagine my joy then when Gary said his friend Esther would like to meet me during my visit. I was simply delighted and Gary said he would arrange the visit.

Esther was elderly at this point and, it must be said, not in good health. Immediately before our proposed visit, the dear lady suffered a stroke and was confined to the hospital. We were very concerned for her of course, though I selfishly could not help but feel disappointed. Shortly before I was due to leave for the U.K. again, Esther was allowed home from the hospital and Gary visited her. He arrived the morning before I was due to leave saying that Esther had given her apologies, but she had sent something for me. I was intrigued as I gingerly opened the large envelope, but could scarcely believe my eyes to discover it contained an original poster of the film *Dangerous When Wet*! I was thrilled beyond words, but if that was not enough, she had signed it – *To Glennyce from Esther Williams.*

We discovered that there are a very small number of these posters left. She had given Gary one, and the remaining few were in her son's possession. It is to this day amongst my most treasured possessions.

CHANNEL CROSSINGS

On reflection, I think I can pinpoint the exact moment I knew life would involve a great deal of travelling. My very first journey out of the U.K. came once more in the shape of a school trip. I had a headmistress who thought only two forms of education were of value, one was to attend University and the other, she insisted, was to travel. She received the Order of the British Empire (O. B. E.) in recognition of pioneering school travel and for many years this brave lady escorted crocodiles of children across Europe.

My first experience with this exciting form of travel was to be a visit to Lugano on the Swiss/Italian border. I was mesmerised by the lake, the heat and the snow-capped mountains, all new to me after living in industrial Manchester. We were staying in a youth hostel, a new and interesting experience, especially at our first sight of this hostel. Astonishingly, on arrival, we saw that the hostel appeared to have giant marshmallows hanging from every window. Totally perplexed, we asked our teachers what on earth they might be. The answer, of course, was duvets.

That evening we entered the dormitory to find these giant marshmallows on every bunk. We were left bemused wondering what on earth happened next. Did we ask for sheets and blankets too, or did we sleep on top or underneath these strange creatures? It must have taken decades for these wonderful duvets to arrive in Britain, where we were destined to soldier on with sheets and scratchy blankets for another generation.

One beautiful morning early into our trip, we headed for the enthralling Funicular, a form of transport which seemed to me to be quite magical, hauling us up the mountainside with ease. This particular mountain was in fact Monte Bre, and the promised view was all we had hoped for and more, truly awesome. Gazing down, we were all fascinated by the town in the valley and Lake Lugano. I was twelve years old and I imagine this must have been a very impressionable age because this view has stayed clear in my memory ever since. After only moments of admiring the view, most of the children poured through the door of a café and shop with whoops of approval. I found myself wandering off a little and discovered a path, presumably for people to walk to a village immediately below.

It was incredibly still out, only the buzzing of insects heard as I stood looking down on rooftops shining in the hot sun. I was instantly aware of how diverse and wonderful the world was, and if this was just one country within reach, how many more wonders awaited me? I had to find out, that was for sure. Several trips followed with my intrepid headmistress at the helm. We visited Italy and Germany, plus seeing much more of Switzerland. By the time I left school in my late teens, I was well and truly hooked by the travel bug, and with a few friends of similar mind, joined the Youth Hostel Association, the world our oyster!

Initially our adventures with the Youth Hostel Association remained within the borders of the United Kingdom. A little later we became bolder and joined the international branch. However, our first venture would be to Derbyshire, a wonderful county for walking, and we organised a route in the Peak District. Several of my friends had entered the nursing profession, and one particular friend, we all agreed, clearly had a stellar career ahead, if for no other reason than her powers of organisation.

This amazing young lady had the entire route mapped out, the hostels and transport booked, plus we all received a list of items we should purchase for our initial foray into the wide outdoor world. First item would have to be a stout pair of walking boots and thick socks. Trying these on, I felt my heart sink. They were so heavy that I had trouble walking up and down the shoe shop floor, never mind the hills of the Peak District. My friend, with her usual briskness, told me it was only a matter of time before I was used to the boots. Try wearing them at home several times before we go, she instructed me.

The great day arrived and we headed off by train from Manchester, full of excitement and feeling intrepid, to say the least. By the time we reach the foot of the steep path that would take us into the hills, I was already feeling a bit weary, my feet heavy, and this did not bode well. I kept silent and on and on we trudged. As the mist came down, I began to feel distinctly uneasy, though eventually the end of the trek appeared in sight and we scrambled down to our first night in a hostel. Exhausted, I simply could not wait until bed time, but as at all hostels, I had my chores to perform before dinner and later bed. For the evening meal, I peeled what appeared to be a whole sack of potatoes before ever being allowed inside to remove my muddy boots and take a wash. I was so tired by the time dinner was served, I felt almost too weary to eat.

At last it was time to sink into the bunk bed and mercifully rest my feet and legs. It felt bliss as I slipped into well-earned sleep. The following day being Sunday, and as we all had to return to work on the Monday morning, we had a much shorter route. Arriving home late Sunday afternoon, I thankfully removed the dreaded boots and went straight to bed, causing my mother some concern. I too had medical connections regarding my career. I worked in a medical research laboratory, a job I absolutely loved, and one made more enjoyable by the lovely staff and chief medical officer for whom I worked for.

I woke on the Monday morning quite unable to move. I could not say which part of my body hurt most, but one thing was for sure, my legs would not even bend to get me out of bed! My mother arrived in the bedroom wondering why I had not risen and informed me I should be late if I did not get a move on. I told her that sadly I was in so much pain and that I could not move, unable to feel my legs at all. Off she went and with relief I descended once more into a deep sleep. I woke sometime later with a figure standing over me and a strong Irish accent asking me where it hurt most. This was our general practitioner, a delightful lady called Dr. Quinn—yes this was the original medicine woman!

After examining me, she asked what I had been doing in the previous two days. She laughed when I told her about my hike. My mother, bless her, had called the medical lab to tell the good doctor that my legs would not move and I was unable to get out of bed. This dear chap had asked for my G.P.'s number, then proceeded to ring her and issue instructions for her to visit me as a matter of urgency, informing her that I was suffering from an unknown form of paralysis. Dr. Quinn turned to my mother and asked if she told him I had walked some thirty miles over the weekend having previously only made it as far as the local shop. My poor mum said no, she omitted to let him have that information.

"Right," said my patient G.P. "I will certainly let him know and he will not be ringing me again in a hurry." Off she went and I sank into the covers wondering if I could ever show my face at work again.

The dear man forgave me, I am happy to announce, and we had a long talk about ambitions and plans for travel. As much as I loved my job, I told him how I longed to visit foreign lands. He kindly gave me his support and said it was now or never, and if I was to travel I should do so whilst still young. Perhaps it was a case of revenge is better served cold, because he did appear to be showing just a little too much encouragement for my plans.

This dear man was Dr. Michael Williams, a prominent research scientist. He held the post of Chief Medical Officer for Imperial Chemical Industries Limited in Manchester, but his main area of interest and inspiration was his research laboratory. We were a cancer research unit and Michael was a very prominent world leader. He attended conferences in many countries worldwide and always returned bursting with ideas.

We held weekly meetings to discuss plans and research and he always fired us with enthusiasm and inspiration. I was, it had to be said, the very junior assistant at that time, and though I admired him greatly there was always a slightly scary element to him. Suddenly, and without warning, he would appear at the laboratory door and roar, "Glenn!" staring sternly as I scuttled towards him. He fooled me every time into thinking I had done something dreadfully wrong, but then inevitably he would pass me a five-pound note and instruct me to go to the local sweet shop and buy everyone a chocolate bar.

Foolishly, I took to imitating him to make the other members of staff laugh. I was good at this, though inevitable one day I would come unstuck. Michael had what we called behind his back his "his London outfit" comprised of a very long, black, double-breasted overcoat, white silk scarf, bowler hat and rolled umbrella—honestly, I am not making this up! One day he was attending a morning meeting, planning to take a trip to London that afternoon, and I took it into my head to try on his London outfit. Michael was six-foot-four and I am five-feet-two inches, so you can see the problem right there.

I stood on a high stool and slipped on the coat, having one of the other girls fasten it for me, and it still reached the floor. I popped the bowler on my head, wound the silk around my neck and clutched the rolled umbrella, and then in his clipped voice announced   I was off to London on the one o'clock train. The girls were helpless with laughter, until suddenly the office door opened and in stepped Michael.

I was in a pretty pickle, since I could not jump down from the stool because the coat was buttoned up and would not allow me too. All I could do was stare red-faced at the astonished chap who turned and walked out again. The girls released me and I scuttled back to the laboratory. Nothing was ever said about it, but years later when I was chatting about the incident with his secretary, she told me he had doubled up with laughter and had left the room to keep a straight face and punish me by not saying a word. We were all subjected to teasing during the time I worked in that wonderful laboratory, and laughter never far away.

Imperial Chemical Industries sprawled over a huge area adjacent to a small village. This village benefitted enormously from the close proximity of such a large workforce. It had a bustling village street leading to the main busy road into the city of Manchester, and as such saw a huge amount of traffic. The laboratories were numerous and varied in their lines of research. I am sad to report that in those days many animals were used in experiments for medical advances. Wonderful breakthroughs were achieved, but I doubt it could have happened this way today. One laboratory contained a group of monkeys and the doctor in charge of this research was an excitable dark Spaniard with a small build.

Walking with friends one day for lunch, we were treated to the amusing sight of the good doctor chasing one of his very nimble monkeys between the laboratory buildings. With amazing speed the monkey, who had clearly bided his time for a quick escape, shot through the main gate and proceeded along the main street of the village. Cars screeched to a halt and passers-by were treated to the sight of this small dark-skinned, very hirsute Spaniard in a white coat chasing a small dark monkey. Indeed, several people were heard to remark you could only identify the doctor by his white coat.

It was a sad day when I left the laboratory and all my jolly companions to head for Los Angeles, feeling confident that it was only a matter of time before Michael and his team had a real breakthrough in cancer research. It was a sad day when only months after my arrival in California I learned Michael had been killed in a traffic accident.

YOU HAVE TO HAVE FAITH!

There were, it needs to be said, many reasons for my desire to travel, encouragement and inspiration from my headmistress being only the first. I had an innate sense of "only being here once" and wanted to make the most of this life I had been given. I also soon realised that if I did want to see the world, I should have to strike out alone.

Many friends expressed an interest in travel, but as soon as I suggested they acquire a passport it all began to feel too real and they backed out with indecent speed. I loved my parents unconditionally, they were good kind people and the best possible parents I could have had. They were, however, very religious and from an early age, like so many of my generation, I would be expected to attend Chapel up to three times a day each Sunday. By the time I reached my teens, I felt in need of respite and it became a priority to see how the rest of the world lived. Learning about the world and other religions proved to be not only fascinating, but rewarding.

The time Audrey delivered little Robbie was in fact Hanukah and it fell to me to encourage the other two boys to watch as I lit the candles on the Menorah, then I listened whilst they said little prayers. During the years I lived with the Greenberg family, I was thrilled to be part of their religious celebrations and rituals. I also met Jehovah

Witnesses at one point whilst in Los Angeles, Mormons too, and they all held a fascination for me.

Many years ahead, I had the most surreal, and almost funny, religious experience in Austria. I had been invited to speak at a conference in Salzburg. The weekend of talks and lectures had been organised by a charismatic, hugely-successful author and broadcaster, a lively man and very devout Roman Catholic named Wulfing von Rohr. The evening before the conference happened to be the Feast of Fatima and I was invited to go with Wulfing to attend a service in honour of Fatima at a little village high in the mountains. I was thrilled to be asked and off we went through the most wonderful scenery imaginable. Higher and higher we went until finally reaching this beautiful little place. The service was to be held in a wonderfully old ornate church in the centre of the village, the entire village aglow with candles. Feeling rather hungry at this point, my new friend suggested we go to the pub for a meal. We went, delighted to discover that this was the very time of the asparagus harvest and the menu reflected that fact. How marvellous the meal was, but it had taken a while to arrive, the village being so busy due to the festival. Suddenly we were in a great hurry and I was pulled by the hand from the pub and round to the side door of the church.

Upon entering this church, I found we were actually in the choir dressing room with the choir, about to enter the corridor leading to the rear of the church. "Tuck in behind," I was told by my smiling companion and, as there did not appear to be any alternative, I did as I was told. Round to the back of the church we processed, catching up with a long line of clergy singing and swinging scented orbs. Scarcely able to believe I was there, I followed this long procession down to the very front of the church, then led up to the very alter where chairs had been placed. It was indicated that I should sit on one of these next to the priest, facing the congregation who looked as confused and bemused as myself!

You could almost hear their thoughts *'Who on earth is she?'* Indeed, why was I there? My mischievous companion was grinning with delight as I struggled for almost an hour and a half to work out when to stand and when to sit. The hymns, to my astonishment, were in English so at least I could sing them with enthusiasm. It was a baptism of fire in the Catholic tradition and an experience not to be forgotten in a hurry.

I have had a brush with a variety of religions over the years and did find most of them fascinating. At one point in my life, much to my amazement, I found myself a member of staff at a theological college. This college was of a denomination new to me, namely Swedenborgianism. The organisation followed the teachings and philosophies of Emanuel Swedenborg, a theologian, philosopher and scientist who had lived some three hundred years previously in Sweden. I found some of the aspects of this religion interesting and inspiring, but never to the point of joining them. I did, however, work at the college for many years and found great support and help from the staff when researching and writing my books.

As is often the case, this particular brand of religion was taken up much more enthusiastically by our American brethren and it flourished there in great numbers compared to the United Kingdom. Shortly after the publication of my first book, the principal of the college, Reverend Ian Arnold, a truly lovely and charismatic man, secured an invitation for me to go to America and speak at a spring festival at the church in Pennsylvania. It all sounded most exciting and when the invitation duly arrived, I accepted at once. It involved travelling to a small town called Bryn Athyn in Pennsylvania and would require some organisation to get there. Recounting the prospect of this trip to my good friend Mary, I was rather surprised when she said, "Can I come with you?"

I assured her that it might involve me working most of the time and perhaps she might be bored. Mary assured me she would not be bored and would find it fascinating— never a truer word said in jest! I agreed that it might be nice to have a travelling companion to the States for once and so readily agreed. Travel arrangements were in place and we studied our route. First, we would arrive in New York, where we would spend one night before travelling by train to Philadelphia. From there we would take a further train to the outskirts of Bryn Athyn, where we had been invited to stay with one of the church families. It all sounded straight forward enough, if a little convoluted, but with great excitement we set off one rainy Manchester night for New York.

I had over the years made several visits to New York, but had never experienced the view travelling at night across the Brooklyn Bridge into the city. This was pure magic, breathtaking displays of light. The familiar skyline we have all seen in countless films and television programmes actually took one's breath away when viewed live. New York was a first-time experience for Mary and we had a superb night in that busy city.

Friday morning dawned and we made our way to the train station for our trip to Philadelphia. Sadly, we did not have a great deal of time to explore this historic city. Gazing at the endless timetables on offer in the station, we were totally confused and it took the two of us considerable time to work out which train would actually get us to where we needed to be. At this point I was grateful for Mary being there to help me with all the complications. At last we boarded the correct train and settled for our journey into the back of beyond, or so it appeared.

We finally arrived at the little station where we had been instructed to alight, and where our hostess for the next few days had promised to meet us. After stepping out of the train, we realised at once that the word 'station' was an optimistic one. It was in fact just a concrete structure in the middle of nowhere.

As our little train disappeared into the distance, we were left with a deafening silence, and nothing in sight for as far as the eye could see. We had in fact been the only two passengers to alight at that point. Desolation appeared to stretch out from all sides, resembling a scene from the "Grapes of Wrath"! Mary and I looked at each other in disbelief, wondering what on earth we should do next, not a car or phone box in sight. This was, of course, long before the days of mobile phones.

After ten minutes or so, we heard a car in the distance, which mercifully drove straight to us and stopped at our feet. It became evident, to our great relief, that this was our hostess. A sweet smiley lady jumped out of the car saying, "My goodness, you did well to find this place. Well done!" We silently added that we also thought we had done well to find such a spot, but smiled warmly in return and gladly piled into her car. What an experience lay ahead, and it proved to be a revelation in the spiritual community of Bryn Athyn, but first I must tell you about the house.

Pulling up outside a rather lovely single-story house, our new friend welcomed us inside, shouting for her husband to come and say hello. Suddenly, a rather jolly-looking man scooted across the polished hardwood floors at great speed towards us. We learned this chap had suffered a stroke and had great difficulty walking. Instead of using a wheelchair indoors, he had an office chair, one of the comfortable types with three wheels underneath, which he discovered, with a push off his good foot, could propel him swiftly across the polished floor. He could scoot the entire length of the house in this manner, able to reach almost any surface.

After a tour of this house, that we noticed sat on the same grounds as a much larger, grander house, visible outside the window on a hill. We were told that the big house had in fact been their family home, but after the children left, and the stroke caused problems, they sold it along with most of the land, retaining an area on which to build their current home. They then told us the amazing fact that this house had been delivered on a lorry! It was entirely flat pack, electrics, water and heating all slotted into place in the matter of a couple of days. Truly amazing, because this lovely house appeared to have been part of the scenery for ages.

After coffee and cake, we were told that we had been invited to the community centre for our evening meal. They asked if we might like to take a walk first, get a little fresh air and have a look around. It was early evening as Mary and I set off for our little walk. There was something surreal about this neighbourhood that we could not quite identify, but Mary observed that there was not a single person anywhere in sight, no traffic at all, not a single shop, restaurant or coffee bar. We began to giggle and decided we had landed either in a time warp or the village of the dammed!

Arriving back at our host's house, we commented about the silence and the lack of shops, and were astonished to hear the reason why. The entire small town was composed of Swedenborgian Church members, and therefore no distractions of any kind had been included. No shops, restaurants, coffee shops, cinema's or gyms, and on and on the list went. However, they had built all the houses, maternity hospitals, nursery schools and all manner of education up to and including a university. They had their own hospital, fire station, ambulance service, funeral service. In short, this community had every stage of life catered from cradle to grave. Every activity was church oriented and totally fascinating to us.

The evening dinner was quite wonderful, the young people of the community serving their elders with good humour and efficiency. We were told this was a Friday night ritual that all looked forward to. It was a special evening, being the start of the festival organised for the weekend, an Angel Festival, and I looked forward—with just a little apprehension about my involvement. I need not have worried; the festival was amazing. The sight that met our eyes proved to be intoxicating as we entered the main hall of the high school, angels as far as the eye could see.

This entire hall was filled with stalls selling angels, displayed for the vast crowds that were rolling up from far and wide. Well beyond the community borders was a fine array of angel crafts. You could purchase angels fashioned from glass, ceramics, iron, silver, gold, wicker, cloth, wood, not to mention angel biscuits and cake. On and on the list went, every variety and type of angel you could possibly imagine. The lecture hall was filled with flowers and had a large stage where I learned I was to give my talk later in the morning. Guest speakers were set from ten A.M. to five P.M. The hall was filled to capacity, hundreds of eager and enthusiastic people filling the seats.

It turned out to be a wonderful experience. At the end of the festival we were invited to the home of the main organiser for a celebratory dinner and we looked forward very much to going, realising that this community, although appearing at first very insular, was in fact comprised of lovely, warm, welcoming people.

The celebratory evening meal was held at a very impressive house with an amazing garden stretching into the distance. It appeared we were joining the organising committee for a debriefing chat, where everyone agreed, quite rightly so, that the festival had been a huge success. Mary and I went swiftly into the dining room where our evening meal was comprised of many varieties of wonderful pizza.

Mary had enjoyed a fabulous day, supporting me by listening to my talk, buying lovely angels, and meeting so many nice people. However, upon entering the dining room, she was rooted to the spot by possibly the most handsome man we had ever seen. We had been told to form a circle around a table when this handsome hunk said to Mary with a twinkle in his eye, "Would you mind if I held your hand?"

Mary positively swooned, thinking all her Christmases had arrived at once. Holding on to her hand, he then instructed everyone else to hold hands whilst he said grace. It turns out he was the minister! "Still, it was a lovely moment whilst it lasted," Mary said.

Later in the evening we all walked to the bottom of the huge garden, where a surprise was waiting for us. There in the sky was the wonderfully bright Hale Bop comet, a perfect end to a wonderful star-studded event.

There was more delight to follow as we made our way back to New York. Val and August had flown from Los Angeles to join us. We had paid for an apartment for several days and this time I was able to see New York from yet another perspective. August had been born and bred in the city and proved to be an excellent guide, taking us to the Italian quarter where he had grown up amongst his Italian family, an area we should never have found by ourselves. Full of delightful shops and restaurants, we tasted Italian food at its very finest.

As we continued to walk, the delights of this city just kept coming. We virtually walked the whole of Central Park, quite a feat, and were both pretty tired by the end of that day. In the days ahead, many interesting visits followed. We visited the fabulous Museum of Modern Art, the Opera House and, of course, we simply had to see a show on Broadway. This turned out to be the fantastic "Chicago" and I should say that I am not at all a fan of musicals, but even I found this superb.

Finally we hit the shops, wandering around the amazing Macy's, window shopping outside Tiffany's and even popping inside Trump Tower. The gold decoration and general bling was a sight to behold and a testament to the fact that no amount of money can buy you good taste. Little did we know however, that in years to come this building and its owner would be dominating our daily lives.

Sadly, the visit came to an end and Mary and I found ourselves flying home on Easter Sunday. Before we left, we briefly attended mass at the wonderful St Patricks Cathedral on Fifth Avenue, filled to capacity with worshipers and the most wonderful singing.

Arriving at the airport for departure, we discovered that one of the perks of flying on Easter Sunday was an almost empty plane. Our cabin crew took full advantage of this fact and put their feet up, instructing us to simply help ourselves to the bar. An unusual flight, to say the least. At one point our pilot announced that if we moved to the left-hand side of the plane there would be an amazing sight. Indeed, there was, because this time our special comet Hale Bop looked almost within touching distance, quite magical seeing it from such a high vantage point. We felt sad to land once more in Manchester, but our thoughts were filled with lovely memories of a very special trip.

THE ITALIAN JOB

Trips to Europe have featured prominently in my life and they have often involved meeting up with Gary for joint ventures and speaking engagements. The city of Turin features in the latest of these trips and will remain prominently in my memory for many reasons. We had, along with many other international speakers, been invited to take part in a festival to be held in a large hotel not far from the Turin airport. This was, of course, popular and convenient for many of the speakers who travelled widely.

I should have known this would be an eventful trip right from the start. The details for travel appeared to be lost on line and only arrived at the last moment. It was late in the day and I realised I would have to change flights at De Gaul airport, a stressful event. It is a huge and rather chaotic airport, a daunting task to navigate one's way around even for someone used to flying the globe for most of her life.

Sitting next to a nervous chap on the outward leg of this journey to Turin, I was surprised when he told me that I did not have enough time to transfer and find my next plane. I assured him I had a whole hour to transfer, but he shrugged and said, "It is clear you have never been to Charles De Gaul airport before." As it turned out, he ended up being absolutely correct.

Landing was sheer chaos, hordes of people dashing every which way, and the directions for my ongoing flight taking me down seemingly never-ending corridors. Time ticked away and I finally found the door I thought led to the next departure gate only to see it led to a transfer bus that would deliver me to yet another part of this vast airport. To be honest, I was rather in a panic at this point, not entirely sure which bus I needed to catch.

Suddenly, a clear, commanding voice said, "Would you let me pass please. I have to catch the plane to Turin and have very little time!" This lady knew exactly where she was going and, with a sigh of relief, I followed her closely. The fact that this lady was tall proved a great help, but more especially the fact that she was wearing a luminous green sweater. Scuttling behind her on a wing and a prayer, we boarded the plane at the very last moment, the doors shutting behind me as I stepped aboard, and off we went.

At last, late in the afternoon, I arrived at the hotel in Turin, delighted to find Gary also emerging from a taxi. An evening meal was to be served at seven, so we said our hello's and went to change for the evening meal. The conference was due to begin that Friday evening, with a lady giving a talk whilst the rest of the presenters were free until Saturday morning. I had the dubious pleasure of being the first speaker at 9:30 A.M.

It proved to be a very enjoyable evening meal, relaxed as I met all the other presenters, when suddenly the lady who had organised this whole festival appeared, saying inspiration had struck in the shape of a lovely idea. She would be pleased if we would all follow her on to the stage where she would like each of us to talk for a few moments about our presentations the following day. "Just a five-minute talk will be fine," she said. "Give the audience a flavour of your themes."

We were a little daunted because people had travelled from all over Europe and the United States and most, I feel sure, had hopes of a fairly early night. Obligingly, we filed into the hall to find the place packed with an audience of around a thousand. We climbed onto the stage, sitting in a semi-circle of twelve presenters. The first lady, an Italian, began to speak and I calculated it would take at least an hour if we each spoke for five minutes. This, however, proved to be supremely optimistic. The dear lady spoke for thirty minutes!

I groaned inwardly as the second presenter took the mike, this lady also speaking for thirty minutes. Oh my, this was grim. It was close to midnight before the mike reached Gary, who was sitting next to me. We were the only two who spoke for five minutes. Finally, bleary-eyed, we staggered to bed at one in the morning, little realising this was a baptism of fire, for this would be conference Italian style!

Presenting myself for duty bright and early the following morning, I was informed by the lady with inspirational ideas that I would not be speaking first after all. Instead, I would be the last speaker before lunch. This required me to appear again in the main hall by 12:30 P.M. I nodded and left the hall for a coffee and eventually the appointed time arrived. I turned up once more to be told that I would not be speaking until four P.M. I was beginning to understand how things were shaping up and Gary laughingly told me that this was Italian timing.

Well, I finally gave my talk toward the end of the day, happy to realise everyone could retire to the dining room for food, chat and relaxation. Sunday dawned and all appeared to be going according to plan. Gary had to leave for Rome after lunch for his next appointment and so we said our goodbyes. I did not have any tasks that afternoon and had been told the festival itself finished at five P.M. My flight home was early Monday morning, so I did in fact have some free time.

I assumed dinner would once more be held at six P.M. and so shortly before the conference finished at five, I went to my room for a little rest. By this time I was actually feeling pretty tired and had a nice lie down. Gazing at the clock, I saw it was six and so gathered my bag and sweater to go downstairs for dinner. To my astonishment, I was greeted by a scene resembling the "Marie Celeste" for the entire hotel was empty, everyone gone, and the dining room firmly locked and shuttered, not even a receptionist in sight!

It appeared everyone had vanished on the stroke of five, speeding off in a cloud of dust. I went outside thinking I should find a little café open for a bite to eat. There was a lovely little place Gary and I had found for coffee earlier, but this was an Italian Sunday and all out-of-town shops were closed. After walking a considerable distance, I realised that I would not find anywhere to eat that night. I walked back to the deserted hotel and ate a packet of biscuits for dinner.

Monday dawned and I found myself back at the airport, once again facing a state of nerves at the thought of the manic transfer ahead of me. Arriving in De Gaul airport, heart sinking, I was decanted with what appeared to be thousands of fellow travellers into this human maelstrom. Trying to decipher the notice board, it became obvious that once more I would have to negotiate the entire length of the airport to find the appropriate gate for departure.

Looking for a place to start, I gazed around the hall, when suddenly, to my great joy, there appeared the tall English lady in her bright green sweater forging her way through the crowd. Uttering a prayer of thanks, I tucked in behind her. We did the whole thing in reverse and once again, thanks to this lady, I found myself reaching the home-bound plane just in time. I was so relieved to land in Manchester, and even managed to have a chat with the lady who had guided me so well. She was lovely and highly-amused, telling me that she did the trip at least once a month, which I thought was so very brave of her. We said our goodbyes and I waved her off, uttering yet again a prayer of thanks for my pea-green angel!

NOT 'PLANE' SAILING!

You may well have gathered that some of the most traumatic moments of my life have taken place in airports. I have travelled a great deal and feel perfectly calm as long as my flight is direct, but whenever I have to transfer it all goes pear shaped! You will also be aware by now that every few years or so I find myself going back to Los Angeles. It certainly is my second home, but over the years there have been so many changes.

Back in the day, California had a wonderful rocky coastline, wide flat valleys filled with extended orange orchards giving way to soaring snow-capped mountains. Each time I returned, the orchards became fewer and fewer, until now the valley area is filled with houses and the oranges are imported from Florida. The snow-capped mountains are often obscured by the dark brown smog, the beautiful views disappearing. Of course, the population has exploded. Recently, the area of Los Angeles County reached a total of ten million people, and the increase of traffic has had the knock-on effect of producing smog, but I think Los Angeles is still beautiful and I feel drawn to this city and its people.

Perhaps my most traumatic airport transfer happened on my way to Los Angeles, and hoping to transfer by way of O'Hare airport in Chicago. I was pretty nervous because I knew this to be one of the largest airports in the world. I was on my way to visit Val, who had become seriously ill. Working in college at that time enabled me to visit during the extended Christmas holidays, allowing me to go see how Val was progressing.

I booked a flight for the 26th of December. This was 1988 and the 21st day of that month witnessed the most horrific incident in airline history the United Kingdom has ever witnessed. This was, as everyone recalls, the Lockerbie disaster. Pan Am Flight 103 from Frankfurt to Detroit via London and New York was destroyed by a bomb, killing all 243 passengers and 16 crew—not terribly confidence boosting to anyone hoping to fly across the Atlantic. So, with great foreboding, I arrived at Manchester airport for my flight to Chicago. It was not an auspicious start to my journey because shortly after checking in there was an announcement saying the flight had been delayed due to bad weather in Chicago.

This proved to be a bit of an understatement because they were in fact experiencing the worst snow storm in a decade. Several hours passed before we were finally allowed to board, but by this point I was pretty sure I had already missed my on-going flight to Los Angeles. I asked the stewardess if I could possibly make the flight, and she simply laughed and said, "I should not concern myself with any flight because nothing has flown out of Chicago for the past three days!"

We were told that it was by no means certain that the plane could land at O'Hare and to be prepared for a diversion. In any event, the pilot decided to try, and so, amid a great deal of buffeting by the strong winds, we did finally manage to land. We could see the swirling snow outside and knew we were in for a cold blast the second the door opened. Even so, we were not prepared for this blast. It looked more like a scene from a polar expedition.

The snow was falling in every direction, including upwards, so thick and fast you simply could not see beyond your nose. An airport transport bus had been driven to the steps of the plane and one by one the passengers were helped off. Two men in yellow snow suits held each person by the arms and struggled to walk them down the steps onto the waiting bus. The wind was so strong that many people had trouble standing upright. I'm still not certain how on earth the pilots landed the plane, hard to imagine.

Eventually the bus was filled with the passengers and we were on our way to the terminal. Once inside, we were smoothly ushered through passport control. Baggage recovery was also a doddle and so I began to think that all would be fine after all. Little was I prepared for the scene that met my eyes on entering the arrivals hall, this more like a scene from a disaster movie! Every available seat and bench, every foot of floor space, was filled with weary would-be travellers. The place was heaving and, as the hostess had said, no one had been out of the airport for three days.

My heart sank as I stood with my suitcase and boarding ticket in hand. Talk about the eternal optimist. Incredibly, at this point, an airport official came up to me, having seen my Los Angeles label on the suitcase, and urgently said, "Be quick, the pilot of the Los Angeles flight has decided to try and take off."

The pilot had apparently been encouraged by the fact that our plane had landed successfully and so thought he would try for the same runway to leave. This woman took my suitcase and told me that she would ensure it was on the plane, but I would have to run if I wanted to catch the flight. That is when the real nightmare began. She quickly gave me instructions of how to get to my leaving gate, and they were the most complicated set of instructions I had ever heard. They went along the lines of, "Go right, take the lift to the third floor, go left, then take the lift to the fourth floor, through the main hall, along the corridor to the main square, down the right lane of gates to number 60. Got it? Go, hurry!"

My head was spinning as I tried to remember the instructions. It was a long way to go and I had a panic attack at one point when I emerged from a lift and found myself in the car park! I had to start again. This time I took off my shoes and ran for my life. I was followed closely behind by an elegant lady in high heels who constantly shouted, "Wait for me!"

I urged her to take the shoes off, but to no avail. Eventually I found the long corridor of numbered gates, but horrified to see I was only at number one. We had to run all the faster to reach 60 and I knew there were only a couple of minutes, if not seconds, to go! The check-in staff saw me running and shouted encouragement, and they almost pushed me onto the flight. The door clanged shut and we were off. I had been bungled into a seat, heart pounding, scarcely able to breathe, or believe I had found my way across that vast airport. The take-off was distinctly hairy, heavy winds tossing the plane every which way, but we were at last air borne and off to Los Angeles.

I finally arrived in Los Angeles at midnight, totally exhausted, and sad that I had to ring August and Val at such a late hour to ask them drive and collect me. Val's voice on the other end of the phone was incredulous, they had been checking the news constantly and informed that no plane had flown out of Chicago, and it would be several days yet before they were back to normal. They hurried to collect me, scarcely believing I had actually flown from Chicago. On seeing me, Val said, not for the first time, "How the hell did you get here!"

REUNION

O ne of the great tragedies of my life was the death of my mother, for whom death came suddenly and far too soon. My daughters were babies and it was so sad to realise she would not see them grow to adulthood. My father was left devastated. He had been looking forward to retirement and all the plans they had made for that time in their life. I remember ringing Sally to tell her the awful news, and she immediately said that as soon as we felt up to it, we must visit her and bring my father too. Touched by her kindness, we said our thanks, and so it was that sometime later we all headed for the airport and a flight to Cleveland, Ohio.

It so happened that Sally and I had married at roughly the same time, and produced two children at the same time. In fact, our daughters had been born just days apart. It was wonderful to be met at the airport by Sally and her husband, and although tired from the flight, we were all very excited. My daughters, then four and two years old, arrived at Sally's house very subdued and Sally worried that they might always be like that. Sipping a welcome cup of tea, we heard Sally's son Bryan say to my daughter Gillian, "Can you tackle?"

Gillian had no idea what he meant, but said yes anyway, and soon they were rolling around on the floor, giggling with delight. It was the start of a wonderful holiday for the children, Bryan and Gillian quickly becoming terrific pals. And, to our delight, our daughters Rachel and Glennyce (yes, Sally had named her daughter Glennyce!) also became great friends.

Sally's father took my dad under his wing. One afternoon, he arrived with the intention of taking him and my husband to see an American football match, which turned out perhaps the most exciting event my dear old dad had ever witnessed—the Cleveland Browns versus the Green Bay Packers. What a spectacle for a still grieving man however. He arrived back home with his eyes shining.

There were many exciting outings planned for the family. We visited a state fair, which was quite wonderful, and rather like being in a film! An Amish village was also rather surreal, though quite wonderful. We were allowed to watch the cheese-making process of these amazing people, marvelling at their clothing and horse traps for transport, certainly a day to remember.

Sally and I took time out to attend a literary lunch in downtown Cleveland. This was a most enjoyable experience and a "women only" event. To our amazement, on leaving the hotel where the lunch had taken place, we found a large crowd in the square outside being addressed by Ted Kennedy!

The holiday provided us with lots of excitement, but perhaps the greatest thrill for the adults was attending the opening night of the Cleveland Orchestra's new season. The concert was to feature Mahler and conducted by Claudio Abbado. As a classical music fan, my husband was especially thrilled by this rare treat. The atmosphere was quite amazing and Sally and I had dressed for the occasion, donning long evening dresses, along with all the other ladies attending that night. It was a sparkly affair and on our arrival home, we discovered the television late-news programme featuring the very concert we had just enjoyed. There on the news, amongst the crowd, we could be spotted climbing the front steps to the Severance hall. What a night!

Today, Sally and I communicate all the time by e-mail and other social media, exchanging photographs of our grandchildren, and it is truly wonderful. However, when are daughters Rachel and Glennyce were in their twenties, we arranged to meet with them in New York for a special reunion. It was amazing to catch up and discover that the girls still enjoyed each other's company just as much as they had at two years old.

Yesterday found me once again at the airport, not to board a plane this time, but to stand at the arrivals hall. I scanned the passengers pouring out from customs, and then I spotted the hat, not a large-brimmed black variety this time, but a jolly straw one, beneath which was the same familiar face peeping out from the small brim.

Breaking into a grin, Val took my arm, saying, "Right, any ideas!"

Thank you for taking the time to read this book. If you enjoyed it, please consider telling your friends or leaving a review on Goodreads or the site where you bought it. Word of mouth is an author's best friend and much appreciated.

Lightning Source UK Ltd.
Milton Keynes UK
UKOW06f0611090717
304912UK00001B/6/P